SIMPLE
FRUIT
GROWING

SIMPLE
FRUIT
GROWING

EDITED BY
Peter Blackburne-Maze

WARD LOCK LIMITED · LONDON

ACKNOWLEDGEMENTS

The publishers gratefully acknowledge Peter Blackburne-Maze for granting permission to reproduce the following photographs: pp. 2, 11, 15, 22, 34, 43, 47, 51, 59, 71, 75, 79, 82, 87, 90 and 94.

All the line drawings are by Pamela Dowson.

Front cover: Mixed fruit, courtesy Harry Smith Horticultural Photographic Collection.

First edition, © Ward Lock, by Roy Genders published 1976

Second edition, first published in Great Britain in 1988
by Ward Lock Limited, 8 Clifford Street
London W1X 1RB, an Egmont Company

House editor Denis Ingram
Text filmset in Bembo
by Hourds Typographica, Stafford

Printed and bound in Portugal by Resopal

British Library Cataloguing in Publication Data

Simple fruit growing. — (Concorde
    gardening).
    1. Fruit-culture
    I. Blackburne-Maze, Peter   II. Series
    634   SB356
    ISBN 0-7063-6627-1

Frontispiece: Tower pots are an excellent way of growing strawberries, for use either where no garden exists, or when advancing them in a greenhouse.

CONTENTS

PREFACE

Growing fruit at home is more popular now than it has ever been. This is not only because interest in gardening in general has increased in leaps and bounds but also because fruit growing itself is so much easier than it used to be.

Undoubtedly the main reason for this is the enormous progress that has been made in the breeding of new and more reliable varieties. Apples are the main fruit to benefit from this but raspberries, strawberries and currants (both black and red) have all got their fair share of new blood. To a lesser extent, so have pears, plums, cherries and gooseberries.

New and better rootstocks for tree fruits have certainly played their part in making it easier to grow fruit at home; principally because of the smaller trees that it is now possible to buy and grow. Apples, pears, plums and cherries have all benefitted from this.

Another factor is the increase in the number of garden centres. People are now more aware that fruit isn't just something that you buy in a greengrocer; you can actually grow it at home. Gardeners are becoming more adventurous and having found that producing a crop of, for example, strawberries is well within their capabilities, they move on to other fruits and find them just as easy.

The increasing number of pick-your-own fruit farms is also having an effect on the popularity of fresh fruit. Fruit farms provide town dwellers with a day's pleasant entertainment in the fresh air of the countryside.

It is not necessary to have an enormous garden to grow fruit. The new, and less vigorous, varieties and rootstocks have made it possible to grow fruit trees quite easily in ridiculously small spaces. You can even grow them in tubs and similar containers with the help of modern training methods and potting composts. The type of training often needed by these more intensive tree forms, such as cordons and espaliers, is clearly something that has to be mastered and carried out correctly. However, to most gardeners this is all part of the fascination and fun of gardening.

Finally, the age of mass communication has put a stop to all the humbug and secrecy that once used to surround fruit growing. There is now no excuse whatever for pleading ignorance of some slightly off-beat aspect of gardening, least of all fruit growing; the answer is usually in the nearest library. Better still, you will find it here – along with everything else you need to know to start you off growing fruit at home.

P.M.B-M.

CHAPTER 1

THE FRUIT GARDEN

ITS PLANNING AND PLANTING

Most people love fruit, especially if it is fresh from the garden and, now more than ever, owing to its high cost in the shops, more and more people are taking a serious interest in growing their own. The high overheads that face the commercial grower make it necessary for him to grow only those varieties which crop heavily, so that many of those fruits of outstanding flavour which do not crop as heavily as others are largely neglected by commercial growers. All too often, if you want to have something out of the ordinary and rarely found in shops, you must grow it yourself.

If you have only a small garden you should grow only those fruits of compact habit. Indeed, there are several apples and pears, normally thought of as fairly large trees, which crop heavily when grown in large pots or tubs. A selection of these may be grown on a terrace or patio, or around the walls of a small courtyard to provide an all-year-round supply of fruit. Among apples, the best for pots or tubs are:

'Discovery'	to mature in late summer
'Ellison's Orange'	to mature in early autumn
'Egremont Russet'	to mature in mid autumn
'Sunset'	to mature in late autumn
'Kidd's Orange Red'	to mature in early winter
'Jonagold'	to mature mid winter–early spring
'May Queen'	to mature mid spring–early summer

All are spur bearing (of which more later), forming their fruits on short spurs and so maintaining a compact habit for many years. The one exception is 'Lady Sudeley', the best of all apples for pot and tub culture, which bears its fruit on short twigs or shoots and so is intermediate between the tip- and spur-bearing varieties. Among pears the following will provide fruit from pots or tubs over a long period:

'Doyenne d'Eté'	to mature in late summer
'Onward'	to mature in early autumn
'Conference'	to mature in mid autumn

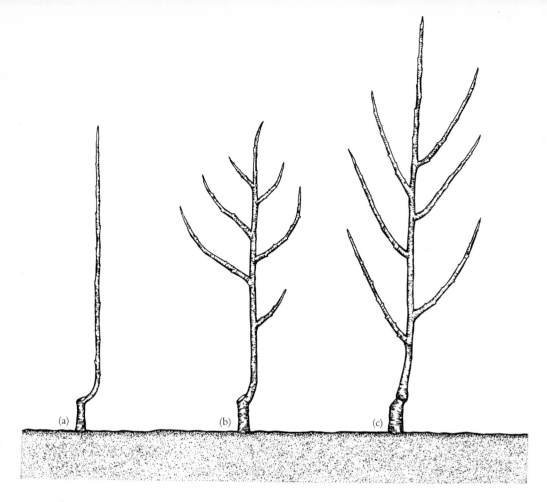

Fig. 1 When bought, fruit trees are usually either (*a*) maiden 'whips', (*b*) feathered maidens or (*c*) two-year-olds.

'Louise Bonne'	to mature in late autumn
'Glou Morceau'	to mature in early winter
'Winter Nelis'	to mature in mid winter
'Josephine de Malines'	to mature in late winter

Pears may also be grown against a sunny wall in espalier form, as horizontal arms which grow out from each side of the main stem, one above the other, each being spaced about 30 cm (12 in) apart. Pears like warmth and should be given the best place in the garden, where the fruit will receive the maximum amount of sunshine to ripen to perfection.

Fig. 2 If the soil or weather are unsuitable for planting newly arrived trees, heel them in until conditions improve.

TYPES OF FRUIT TREE

Dessert plums should be given a similar position, especially the gages which are the most delicious of them all when eaten straight off the tree.

Apples are hardier and may be grown in less select places. Most can be grown as single stem oblique cordons but this system is not suitable for tip-bearing varieties such as 'Worcester Pearmain'.

Cordons should be spaced 1 m (3 ft) apart and are ideal for planting alongside a path or to divide one part of the garden off from another.

Train the stems along stout canes fastened to horizontal galvanized wires.

They come into bearing quickly, as do trees grown as dwarf pyramids: a particularly suitable form for small gardens since they will produce more fruit for the amount of ground they occupy than any other tree.

Standard trees are only grown today in large gardens or where their amenity value is more important than the fruit. Half-standards are really the largest worth considering and they can make excellent specimen trees in lawns or towards the back of mixed or shrub borders.

Very few trees present a lovelier sight than the pink or white blossom of an apple tree in the spring and, of course, you have the fruit as a bonus' in the autumn. Of outstanding beauty when in bloom is 'Arthur Turner', a fine culinary apple. Also outstanding in bloom is 'Annie Elizabeth', the best of all long-keeping cookers and, being late flowering, it is a valuable apple for frost-troubled gardens. Likewise the latest of all apples to bloom, 'Crawley Beauty', is a long-keeping, dual-purpose apple.

Pears come earlier into bloom and plums earlier still. Pear blossom is white against which the dark brown anthers are conspicuous. Besides their blossom and beauty of fruit, they are handsome in leaf, the foliage of that excellent, but very vigorous, variety 'Beurré Hardy' turning brilliant scarlet in autumn; that of 'Josephine de Malines' vivid yellow.

Until quite recently, cherries grew into trees that were far too big for all but the largest gardens and you needed more than one tree so that cross pollination could take place. This put them beyond the range and interest of most gardeners. Now, however, less vigorous rootstocks are available for cherries and the variety 'Stella' will set fruit with it's own pollen. This combination could bring cherries back into the garden but the problem of birds eating the fruit whilst still unripe has yet to be overcome.

CLIMATIC CONDITIONS

Climate is an important consideration when planning the fruit garden. Apples do better in the north than either plums or pears but there are varieties which bear well in cooler districts and those which prefer warmer areas. Some require the drier eastern side of Britain; others the moister atmosphere of the west. Those apples enjoying a cool dry climate are 'James Grieve' (the best pollinator for 'Cox's Orange'), 'Newton Wonder', 'Lord Derby', 'Miller's Seedling' and 'Bramley's Seedling', whilst in a moister climate plant 'Grenadier', 'Laxton's Superb', 'Cox's Orange Pippin' and 'Greensleeves'. These four apples crop better south

Although probably the best dessert apple available, 'Cox's Orange Pippin' is far from easy to grow well and needs good growing conditions.

of a line drawn from Chester to the Wash and are grown widely on a commercial scale.

Pears require similar conditions to the more choice apples but even so, although the English apple stands comparison with any in the world, rarely does the English pear unless the summer and autumn is dry and warm for its ripening. In Britain, 'Jargonelle', 'Beurré Hardy' and 'Durondeau' will crop quite well at almost 330 m (1000 ft) above sea level whilst 'Conference', 'Onward' and 'William's Bon Cretien' require a more sheltered garden and 'Glou Morceau' and 'Doyenne du Comice' even greater warmth to crop and ripen well.

For cold, windswept gardens, 'Winston' is an apple which usually does well and if its fruits were larger it would have been more widely planted commercially. Damsons also do well and may be planted as a windbreak or as a hedge, planting them in a double row 1.25 m (4 ft) apart and allowing 2 m (6 ft) between the trees in the rows. They are handsome in blossom and crop heavily most years.

For a cold north wall, the Morello cherry may be grown in the fan-trained form, the method used for all the stone fruits, including the peach. Being so hardy, it will crop where no other fruit will grow. Or plant gooseberries as cordons, for this is another fruit which enjoys cool conditions.

FRUITS FOR SUCCESSION

Strawberries can be planted beneath gooseberries for they appreciate the shelter from cold winds when in blossom and do well in dappled shade. If gooseberries are planted 1.6 m (5 ft) apart, between the rows there will be room for a double row of strawberries. For early crops, these may be covered with cloches or with a continuous tunnel made of polythene sheeting stretched over hoops.

The gooseberry is the first of the fruits to crop and amongst the first to mature are 'Whitesmith' and 'May Duke', the latter so good for culinary use.

Then come the strawberries. One of the earliest and best flavoured of all is 'Cambridge Vigour'. The well known and popular 'Cambridge Favourite' follows 'Vigour' but this is slowly giving way, with many commercial growers, to the better flavoured Belgian variety 'Hapil'.

The excellent flavoured 'Royal Sovereign' is seldom grown these days. It is very prone to Grey Mould disease of the fruits and the plants are frequently attacked by virus. A good alternative for flavour is the slightly later Dutch variety 'Tenira'.

The so-called autumn fruiting varieties are becoming very popular nowadays. In fact, they are perpetual fruiting but the technique is to de-blossom the plants until early summer. The flowers that are produced from then on are allowed to remain to give fruit in the autumn.

If the plants are protected with cloches from early autumn, they will carry on fruiting until late autumn.

Where no real garden exists, strawberries can still be grown using barrels or special strawberry tubs or tower pots. Even growing-bags may be used very successfully, especially if placed at the base of a warm, sunny wall.

As the summer strawberries are ending, the raspberry crop begins. It has a much shorter season than the strawberry though there are varieties which continue cropping until autumn and, for the amount of ground the plant occupies, it bears more heavily than any fruit. It requires a soil retentive of moisture and unlike the strawberry which will crop well on light land, it does best in a heavy loam. In this respect it is like the black currant which enjoys entirely opposite conditions to the gooseberry both as to soil and climate. Black currants require a mild climate and, whereas gooseberries like dry conditions, currants prefer a moister atmosphere, hence the largest plantations are found in the west country and in Worcester and Hereford. Where raspberries fruit only on the previous season's wood (except for the autumn-fruiting varieties), black currants fruit both on the old and new wood so that the plants require large amounts of nitrogen to enable them to form a continual supply of new wood. If planted 1.6 m (5 ft) apart each way, strawberries may be grown in rows between them so as to make the best use of the land but raspberries are best grown in rows by themselves on one side of the fruit garden, possibly planting a dozen canes of each of, say, three varieties to extend the season.

The first to ripen are 'Malling Promise' and the Scottish variety 'Glen Clova'. These start fruiting in early summer and will carry on until mid summer. Of the two, 'Promise' is probably the better for gardens as the flavour for dessert is less acid than 'Glen Clova'.

A good one to follow these is 'Malling Admiral', which starts fruiting about two weeks later and goes on until late summer. It is excellent for both freezing and dessert and, where there is only room for one variety, this is probably the one to go for. The latest of the summer varieties is 'Malling Leo'. It crops through mid and late summer.

We then move into the autumn-fruiting raspberries. For many years 'Zeva' was the best garden variety but a new one, 'Autumn Bliss', was introduced in 1986 and this crops much more heavily, without sacrificing the flavour. 'Autumn Bliss' fruits from late summer until mid autumn; 'Zeva' starts later but carries on into late autumn. Thus, with raspberries and strawberries, it is now possible to enjoy five months of fruiting so that if the early crops are caught by frost or spoiled by rain, this will not be the finish for that season as was the case in earlier years.

Fruiting from mid to late summer, the tayberry resembles the raspberry in that it fruits only on last year's canes, these being cut out after fruiting. The sunberry also fruits at this time. It is similar to the tayberry in that it is excellent for freezing and jamming. To follow in early and mid autumn is the thornless blackberry, 'Oregon', with its handsome fern-like foliage which should be planted against a trellis or rustic work used to make a cordon. Yields of 4.5–5.5 kg (10–12 lbs) of fruit from a single plant are not uncommon. In fruit at the same time is the vigorous 'Himalaya Giant' which bears enormous crops on both the old and new wood.

For the true blackberry flavour, you should grow 'Ashton Cross'.

Here is a list of reliable soft fruits to provide a long season of picking. Size of garden and ground available will determine how many of each and how many varieties can be planted.

Fruit	Variety	Distance Apart	Season
Blackberry	'Bedford Giant'	3.6 m (12 ft)	mid to late summer
	'Ashton Cross'	3.6 m (12 ft)	mid to late summer
	'Oregon Thornless'	1.8 m (6 ft)	early autumn
	'Himalaya Giant'	4.6 m (15 ft)	early autumn
Black Currant	'Mendip Cross'	1.5 m (5 ft)	mid summer
	'Wellington XXX'	1.5 m (5 ft)	mid summer
	'Ben Lomond'	1.5 m (5 ft)	mid summer
	'Ben Sarek'	1.2 m (4 ft)	late summer
	'Jet'	1.5 m (5 ft)	early autumn
Gooseberry	'Whitesmith'	1.2–1.5 m (4–5 ft)	early summer
	'Keepsake'	1.2–1.5 m (4–5 ft)	early summer
	'Invicta'	1.5 m (5 ft)	early summer
	'Careless'	1.2–1.5 m (4–5 ft)	early summer
	'Leveller'	1.2–1.5 m (4–5 ft)	mid summer
Tayberry		3.6 m (12 ft)	late summer

'Discovery' is replacing 'Worcester' as the main early dessert apple. It is more reliable, has a better flavour and keeps longer.

Fruit	Variety	Distance Apart	Season
Loganberry	'Thornless' (LY654)	2.4 m (8 ft)	late summer
Sunberry		4.6 m (15 ft)	late summer
Raspberry	'Malling Promise'	40 cm (16 in)	mid summer
	'Glen Prosen'	40 cm (16 in)	mid summer
	'Glen Moy'	40 cm (16 in)	mid summer
	'Glen Clova'	40 cm (16 in)	late summer
	'Malling Admiral'	40 cm (16 in)	late summer
	'Malling Leo'	40 cm (16 in)	late summer
	'Autumn Bliss'	40 cm (16 in)	early autumn
Red Currant	'Jonkheer van Tets'	1.2–1.5 m (4–5 ft)	late summer
	'Red Lake'	1.2–1.5 m (4–5 ft)	late summer
Strawberry	'Cambridge Vigour'	38 cm (15 in)	early summer
	'Cambridge Favourite'	38 cm (15 in)	early summer
	'Gorella'	38 cm (15 in)	early summer
	'Hapil'	38 cm (15 in)	early summer
	'Maxim'	38 cm (15 in)	mid summer
	'Tenira'	38 cm (15 in)	mid summer
	'Aromel'	38 cm (15 in)	autumn
	'Gento'	38 cm (15 in)	autumn

Do not plant soft fruits too close together, simply because they are small when received from the nursery. Gooseberries and black currants especially, soon spread out to form bushes 2 m (6 ft) across. Allow them room to develop and until they have grown large, plant strawberries (or vegetables) between the rows. When you are advised to plant a type of fruit at a specific distance between plants, do not try to be clever by planting closer; there is a very good reason for the recommended figure.

SOIL REQUIREMENTS

Most fruits are accommodating as to soil and although raspberries and black currants prefer a heavy soil, they will crop well in a light soil which contains plenty of humus. Most soft fruits require a humus-laden soil, though apart from blackberries and black currants, they do not require large amounts of manure. These two fruits do, because they fruit both on the old and new wood and, bearing fruit and producing new wood at the same time, they require plenty of nourishment. Soft fruits also need humus to conserve moisture in summer for it is during the drier months that they fruit. Incorporate plenty of humus-forming materials before planting. Use material from the compost heap; peat; decayed leaves and lawn mowings; or farmyard manure. Garden compost and farmyard manure have the advantage over other forms of humus in that they contain the nitrogen so essential for the plants to make new growth and it is slowly released over a long period. Other forms of organic nitrogenous manures are poultry manure and fish meal which should be used with those humus-forming materials which contain little plant food. If you live near the coast you will find that chopped seaweed has a similar nitrogen and potash content to poultry manure. Gooseberries and strawberries are lovers of potash and this may be supplied as wood and bonfire ash which has been stored dry so that the potash content will not have been washed away. Potash is also present in fish meal and poultry manure. Farmyard manure also contains a small amount of potash.

After digging the ground and working in the bulky organic matter as you proceed, very heavy soil may benefit from a dressing of garden lime to help form a surface tilth. This, however, should only be added where there is no risk of making the soil too alkaline. Fruit prefers a slightly acid soil; this can be determined by using one of the several inexpensive soil test kits available.

If you are planting in a new garden, especially one that was previously grassland, it is often advisable to treat the land after digging with lindane dust or a specific soil insecticide to destroy any wireworm present.

Whilst these pests are not directly damaging to the roots of fruit trees and bushes, they will certainly attack a wide range of vegetable root crops, especially potatoes.

The ground must be free of perennial weeds before planting fruit and it is imperative to clear the ground thoroughly at this time as it is almost impossible to do so after planting when the plants become an entangled mass of weeds which eventually chokes them to death. Planting in clean, well nourished ground is the first essential in fruit growing.

Land that is of a shallow nature, with no more than 5–7 cm (2–3 in) of top soil overlying a chalky subsoil, may be brought into more suitable condition by 'green' manuring, in addition to deep digging and working in plenty of garden compost or manure. The method is to sow rape seed thickly over the surface. This is done in late summer so that it quickly germinates and it is dug as deeply as possible into the soil when about 7.5 cm (3 in) tall. Both the 'green' top and the mass of fibrous roots will add valuable humus and increase the depth of soil. If the surface is dressed with compost before digging, this will be of additional value.

Neither greenhouse nor frame nor propagator are necessary for fruit growing. Strawberries are increased by runners, and raspberries by the formation of new canes each year. Gooseberries and currants are readily propagated from hardwood cuttings rooted in trenches of sandy soil. Most fruit crops are of a permanent nature and, once planted, all that is necessary to keep them healthy is the judicious removal of old wood.

The use of cloches will, however, extend the strawberry season. The earliest varieties such as 'Cambridge Vigour' may be covered with cloches in late winter, when the fruit will be ripe by late spring. The autumn-fruiting varieties will ripen their fruit until early winter in the south if covered with cloches in mid autumn. Only cover plants in their first fruiting season, after this they are too large and leafy.

Vines may also be grown under cloches, training the shoots formed just above soil level in opposite directions, covering them during the latter weeks of summer and early autumn whilst the grapes are ripening and before the cloches are used to cover late strawberries.

FREEZING

Many soft fruits are excellent for freezing and each year, new varieties are introduced specially for the purpose. It is essential for them to retain their shape and eating qualities after they have been frozen for twelve months and some older varieties do not do this. The deep freeze is most valuable for those fruits which are produced during 'glut' periods, so that none need be wasted. They must however, be frozen when in the peak of condition.

Fruits required for deep freezing should be picked just before they are fully ripe. To allow them to become over-ripe will mean they will become 'mushy' before they are frozen. Gooseberries present no problem but blackberries, strawberries and raspberries should be put individually on trays and then placed in the deep freezer to become partially frozen so that they retain their shape when removed. They are then placed in the polythene bags and put back in the freezer with the minimum delay where they will keep at least a year in perfect condition. They will need 2–3 hours to thaw before using.

Some fruits freeze better than others. In strawberries, 'Cambridge Vigour', 'Favourite' and 'Totem' are particularly good. Among raspberries, 'Malling Jewel', 'Glen Clova' and 'Malling Enterprise' freeze well; avoid 'Malling Delight'. Among black currants, 'Mendip Cross', 'Cotswold Cross' and 'Wellington XXX' are excellent, the fruits having thicker than average skins. Loganberries, tayberries and sunberries freeze well since they have a core. Among blackberries, 'Himalaya Giant' and 'Oregon Thornless', retain their shape and quality after picking and freeze extremely well.

CHAPTER 2

STRAWBERRIES

To quote Isaac Walton: 'Indeed we may say of angling as Dr. Boteler said of strawberries: "Doubtless God could have made a better berry but doubtless God never did".' But in Walton's day, it was the wild strawberries that were so much enjoyed in early summer. They were small but sweet and juicy though they had but a short season. Today, there are varieties to extend the growing season from late spring (under cloches) until early winter in the more favourable districts, covering the plants with cloches in mid autumn. Where no cloches are available, strawberries may be enjoyed from early summer in the south, until the mid autumn, thus giving a greatly extended season compared with pre-war days when they cropped only in early summer in the south, mid summer in the north, and adverse weather could spoil the entire crop. Of all soft fruits grown today, the area given over to strawberries amounts to half the total but most is given to those which freeze and can well.

SOIL REQUIREMENTS

Strawberries prefer a light, well-drained soil, fenland soil, or one of a sandy nature especially. Of all fruits, their blossom is most prone to frost damage. For low-lying land where late frosts persist, plant only the resistant varieties for early crops, such as 'Cambridge Vigour'. Nor are strawberries a reliable crop in excessively wet areas, for the soft fruit, held just above soil level, is often spoilt by soil splashing, and decays with too much moisture. The best varieties for areas of high rainfall are 'Cambridge Favourite' and 'Rival', both of which hold their glossy-skinned fruits well above the foliage, making ripening (and picking) easier in a sunless summer, besides the fruits being well above the soil. But whereas the strawberry must be removed as soon as ripe, whatever the weather, the gooseberry and black currant may be left on the plants until conditions are more suitable for their picking. Again, strawberries are difficult to keep clean of weeds for they have a creeping matted habit and it is no use planting them in weedy land.

A light soil will warm more quickly in spring and the plants will be stimulated into growth sooner than where growing in heavy soil. Also, it will not become too consolidated whilst the fruit is being picked. Again, light land will be well drained in winter and this will reduce the risk of red core root rot which gives the plants a stunted appearance and greatly reduces their cropping before they die back altogether.

If the soil is not too well drained, work in some shingle and peat and when digging the ground, incorporate plenty of compost, decayed leaves and lawn mowings, also straw which has been composted with an activator. Varieties resistant to red core should always be planted in heavy soil and these include most of the Cambridge varieties such as 'Rival' and 'Vigour' for early crops; 'Red Gauntlet' and 'Talisman' for later. They should also be planted a month earlier than where growing in light land, to become well established before winter.

Strawberries require a balanced diet, as they take from the soil nitrogen, phosphorus and potash in equal amounts. Farmyard manure contains each of these foods, as does straw composted with an activator and to which some poultry manure has been added. Remember that the lighter the soil the more potash will be required. Balanced, inorganic fertilizers, such as Growmore, are also perfectly suitable. These fertilizers are raked into the surface before planting.

Strawberries also crop best in slightly acid soil so that peat can be used generously, but though it provides valuable humus it contains no plant food. It should therefore be used with farmyard manure or poultry manure, or with those plant foods previously described. Plenty of humus and plant food is the secret of success with strawberries and the land must be in good 'heart' at planting time. Strawberries do well following a crop of potatoes which will leave the soil in a fine tilth.

A big advantage the strawberry has over other fruits is that it will crop heavily within nine months of planting, that is if the soil has been well prepared. Gardeners of old would plant in mid autumn and disbud the first year, to build up a strong plant to crop heavily the following year but this is not necessary. If planting is carried out from mid summer to early autumn, there will be good crops the following summer. Then, if the plants are kept free of runners, they will conserve their energies, making large plants to bear double the fruit the following year.

PLANTING

If the soil is heavy and the land not too well drained, it will be advisable to plant in raised beds made 1.25–1.5 m (4–5 ft) wide so that picking the fruit may be done from either side without treading the beds. Three rows are planted, allowing about 60 cm (2 ft) between the rows and spacing the plants 40 cm (15 in) in the rows.

In a light loam, plant on the flat, giving the same spacing. Too close planting will encourage mildew, especially in the west where a more humid atmosphere prevails.

Those plants in rows should be kept free of runners for the first two years after planting. They may be allowed to form runners the next year and these are removed in early autumn and a new plantation made, the old plants being destroyed, for strawberries will only crop well for three years at the most, after which new plantings should be made in fresh ground.

Plants in raised beds are allowed to form runners which will fruit the following year and the beds are left down for two or three years before being removed. It is not advisable to plant in beds those varieties which make plenty of leaf for fear of an outbreak of mildew which may happen if the plants are too close together.

When planting new strawberry plants, whether you have raised them yourself or bought them, they should be from runners that grew during the current growing season. These plants are called 'maidens'. The most vigorous are from the runners that are nearest the parent plants.

Although the runners will root naturally into the surrounding soil, a better method is to peg them into 7.5 cm (3 in) pots of used seed compost. They root quicker and the resulting plants can be planted without disturbing the roots.

Always purchase the original stock from a grower who guarantees 'Certified Plants'. This means that they have been inspected by an official of the Ministry of Agriculture and certified as virus-free stock. If sent any distance, they will be wrapped in cellophane with the roots in damp moss for the runners must not be allowed to dry out. The roots must be kept moist so that the plants will get away to a good start. This is especially important where planting early-fruiting varieties.

If planting in early autumn, the soil will usually be in a friable condition but never plant into wet, sticky ground, nor when there is frost in the soil. Use a trowel for planting and make the rows running north to south to ensure the even ripening of the fruit. Spread out the fibrous roots; plants will never do well if the roots are bunched together, but do not plant too deeply. Like most soft fruits, strawberries are surface rooting and never do well if planted deeply: hence they may be grown in shallow soils, provided that the drainage is good and the soil fertile. Use a garden line when planting for it is important that the rows have the correct spacing, not only to allow the plants room to develop but for a hand or mechanical hoe to be taken between the rows to suppress weeds without going too close to the plants.

Plant firmly, treading in the plants and if frost is experienced soon

afterwards, it is advisable to go along the rows when the soil is friable again, to tread in any loosened plants. In a dry autumn, it will be advisable to water in the plants and to give further waterings until established.

BRINGING ON THE CROP

Early in spring, hoe between the plants to break up the surface soil to allow air and moisture to reach the roots and in mid spring, if the spring is cold, give a light top dressing 14 g per sq. m ($\frac{1}{2}$ oz per sq. yd) between the rows with sulphate of ammonia to stimulate the plants into growth. This should be applied on a showery day when it will be immediately washed into the soil.

By mid spring, under normal conditions, plants of early fruiting varieties, such as 'Vigour' and 'Pantagruella', will be forming blossom and a hard frost at this time may blacken the blossom and put paid to any crop that year. Later varieties e.g. 'Domanil' and 'Tenira', will often escape altogether. It is therefore advisable to plant a row of each of four or five varieties with different flowering and fruiting times so as to spread the risk.

Soon after the blossom has set, the plants are given a mulch of clean straw to conserve moisture and prevent soil splashing on to the fruit. Put down a slug repellent or first water the ground with Slugit for the pests can devour a lot of fruit in a single night and make it most unsightly. Damp paper may also be used between the rows or mats made of bitumenized paper, which are quite inexpensive. Whatever material is used, it must be in position before the fruits begin to ripen, which in the south will be during the first days of early summer; about two weeks later in the north. As soon as the fruit begins to swell, it will colour rapidly and the plants will need to be picked over frequently.

Late spring and early summer generally form the driest part of the year and at this time, whilst the fruit is swelling, the plants may need additional supplies of moisture. In dry weather, unless the ground contains plenty of humus to hold moisture, the fruits will not swell to any size and will ripen hard and seedy. It is therefore important to water them frequently and this is best done in the evening so that the moisture will penetrate to the roots during the night. When watering, always give the soil a thorough soaking.

When the fruit is beginning to turn red, watering is withheld for a day

Opposite: Covering the ground with straw is the traditional way of preventing mud from splashing onto ripening strawberries, and also reduces diseases.

or two until the ripe fruit is removed. Then water again if the soil is dry. In this way the fruit will be dry when gathered and will freeze better, whilst the berries will keep their shape if used fresh.

The plants will also benefit from an occasional watering with dilute liquid manure, purchased in bottles as a proprietary make, or it may be made by immersing a sack half filled with manure, in a barrel or tank and leaving it for a week or two. After removal of the sack, fill up the tank with water and use as required.

After fruiting, clear the ground of straw if this has been used to keep the fruit clean, and compost it. Also, remove the leaves from the plant with shears. The new foliage will soon grow from the crown of the plant. Then give the plants a dressing of Growmore and you will have an even bigger crop from the second-year plants.

When to remove the plants will depend upon their continued health and vigour and the variety. Most will crop for three seasons, maybe four if you look after them.

Early fruit, from late spring, can be enjoyed if the early varieties (or some of them) are covered with cloches. Glass barn type or continuous polythene tunnels are suitable, for both cover ground 50–60 cm (20–24 in) in width so that the foliage is not crowded together, which would encourage mildew. For this reason, mildew-resistant varieties and those which do not make excess leaf should be planted for cloching. Strawberries are hardy plants and require the winter months to get a good soaking and recover from their heavy cropping of the previous summer. Give the plants a teaspoonful of sulphate of potash each before the cloches are placed over them in late winter. If the soil is dry, give it a soaking around the plants. By early spring, the sun will be increasing in strength and the plants will need ventilation on warm days. This is done by raising a cloche or two along the row to allow more air to enter during daytime. The cloche should be in place again before evening.

In mid spring the plants will come into flower and should be given ventilation every sunny day to prevent the temperature rising too high. This will also allow bees and other pollinating insects access to the flowers.

Little watering will be required as the comparatively narrow width of the cloches will allow rainwater to soak in from the sides. However, a good look-out should be kept for pests and diseases as these will spread like wild-fire in the confined atmosphere under the cloches.

By late spring, the fruit will be ready to pick and it will be advisable to look over the plants every other day, removing the cloches only to pick the fruit. When cropping finishes, remove the cloches and keep the plants well watered through the summer.

AUTUMN-FRUITING STRAWBERRIES

Cloches are also used to cover the perpetual or autumn-fruiting straw-berries during mid to late autumn. They may be planted as late as mid spring, for the blossom is removed until early summer, during which time a large plant is formed. Mulch and feed the plants in the same way as for the ordinary varieties. In a dry, sunny autumn they will ripen large quantities of fruit even without cloching but cloches are necessary to continue the cropping. They do especially well in the south.

The method of growing is to plant a double row 45 cm (18 in) apart, which will permit them to be covered by a barn cloche. Space the plants 45 cm (18 in) in the rows and allow them to form runners which will also bloom and fruit in autumn by which time the beds will have become a mass of plants all bearing fruit. The soil must be well prepared before planting otherwise the fruit will be small. Keep the plants well watered throughout summer and, from mid summer, give them a watering with liquid manure in alternate weeks to build up strong plants by the end of summer when they begin to fruit. If the autumn is cold and wet, cover the plants in early autumn. Usually autumn is a dry, sunny time of year and if summer strawberries fail, the autumn varieties will compensate. It is excess moisture rather than cold which causes the fruit to decay, and it is botrytis that mostly troubles the autumn strawberries. Allow the cloches to remain open at each end of the row to allow a free circulation of air which will keep the plants and the fruit dry.

The plants die down completely after fruiting and early in spring when they begin to grow again, remove the older plants from the beds (they will no longer be in neat rows), allowing the runners, some of which have already fruited, to remain to fruit again. Those in turn will send out more runners which will fruit in autumn. It is necessary however, to feed the plants well during spring and summer, otherwise they will impoverish the soil and the fruit will be small and hard. Do them well and you will be rewarded a hundredfold. The fruit can be used fresh and it freezes well.

GROWING IN BARRELS AND TUBS

Strawberries may be grown in barrels and tubs into which holes of 2.5 cm (1 in) diameter are drilled and spaced 40 cm (16 in) apart. A small courtyard or verandah could take several tubs (barrels cut in half across the middle). They are of oak and are long lasting. Planting is done in the holes around the tub, also at the top and if several are used, each may be planted with a separate variety to provide a succession of fruit through

'Cambridge Favourite'. For many years the main commercial and home variety. It is a reliable and heavy cropping second-early.

summer. 'Cambridge Vigour' and 'Hapil' do well in tubs.

First place at the bottom of the tub, which must have drainage holes, an 8 cm (3 in) layer of crushed bricks or crocks, then a layer of coarse peat or bark for drainage. The tub is then filled up with fresh loam into which has been incorporated some moist peat and some decayed manure. Mix well together before adding a handful of bone meal and one of sulphate of potash, again mixing it well. After filling and firming, set the plants 15 cm (6 in) apart at the top and where the holes are. Planting is done in autumn when several pickings of fruit will be enjoyed the following summer with larger amounts next year. Remember, never allow the plants especially in the side holes, to lack moisture and when making new leaf in spring and setting the fruit, it may be necessary to give the tubs a soaking twice weekly but never so much as to percolate through the drainage holes.

The plants will respond to an occasional watering with dilute liquid manure after the fruit has set.

VARIETIES

EARLY
'PANTAGRUELLA' The earliest of all, producing good crops of nicely flavoured berries. Good for cloching or forcing in a greenhouse. May need frost protection outdoors. Tender-skinned so not popular with commercial growers. Small and compact plants.
'CAMBRIDGE VIGOUR' Grows well on chalky or limestone soils. Very good flavour. Good for use under cloches and for forcing. Best grown for one year only; subsequent crops are later and the berries smaller.

MIDSEASON
'CAMBRIDGE FAVOURITE' The most widely grown commercial variety. Produces plenty of runners. Good for processing. Moderate flavour. Crops well for six years or more. Fruit stays in good condition for some days on the plants when ripe.
'HAPIL' Likely to replace 'Favourite' as the most widely grown variety. Better colour. Firmer. Will crop for at least four years. Bears well on light soils and under dry conditions. Very good flavour.
'TOTEM' The best processing variety. Rather poor yield in first year but improves with age. Especially good for freezing as it holds it's shape well when thawed. Bright red inside.
'ELSANTA' A new Dutch variety that is still in short supply. One of the best-looking berries: firm, well-shaped, bright-red and shiny. Good flavour.

LATE

'BOGOTA' The latest summer variety. Best kept for only one year as fruit size and shape deteriorates with age. Moderate flavour and yields.

'TENIRA' Excellent appearance and flavour but fruits tend to be small after first year.

AUTUMN FRUITING (perpetual).

'AROMEL' Very good flavour. Crops well from late summer to mid autumn. Best cropped for one year.

'GENTO' Largest fruits of the perpetuals. Crops twice: in summer and again in autumn. Good flavour and crops. Succeeds well on chalky soils.

'OSTARA' Good crops from late summer onwards. Medium-sized fruits of good colour. Good flavour.

CHAPTER 3

RASPBERRIES

Raspberries are our chief provider of soft fruit after the main strawberry crop is over, and they possess a unique flavour. The fruits freeze well and make excellent jam, though the advent of the freezer has meant that few people have any surplus fruit for preserving. As with the strawberry, there are now varieties which will spread the season over many weeks so that a period of wet weather, which may spoil the fruit of one variety, does not mean the destruction of the whole crop. As the canes grow upright, to about 2 m (5–6 ft) above soil level, picking the fruit is easier than with strawberries and, once planted, if well looked after, a plantation will remain in bearing for up to twelve years, and no hardy plants bears more fruit for the amount of garden space it occupies.

Flowering later than the strawberry, most varieties of raspberry miss the late frosts, but the canes should be protected from cold winds if the garden is exposed. This may be done by erecting interwoven fencing around the fruit and vegetable garden or by planting a hedge of *Cupressocyparis leylandii*, spacing the plants 90 cm (3 ft) apart and in three to four years they will have reached a height of 2 m (5–6 ft). Strong winds blowing directly on to the raspberries may cause the canes to break, with a reduction in the following season's crop.

If the garden is in a frost hollow, it is advisable to reduce risk from frost damage to a minimum and to grow the later flowering varieties such as 'Malling Jewel', and 'Norfolk Giant', which will fruit in that order, with 'Autumn Bliss' to provide fruit in autumn. Though 'Malling Jewel' blooms early, it is frost resistant whereas 'Malling Promise', which blooms at the same time, is rather prone to frost damage.

Plant raspberries along one side or at one end of the fruit garden, preferably with the cane rows oriented north-south to ensure the even ripening of the fruit.

SOIL REQUIREMENTS

The raspberry enjoys a soil capable of retaining summer moisture, but also one which is well-drained in winter. A heavy loam is ideal and if the soil is light and sandy, incorporate plenty of humus in autumn before planting. Peat is valuable to hold moisture in dry weather, as is garden compost and farmyard manure. Of all soft fruits, raspberries detest drought and will produce only weak, thin canes and small seedy fruit unless well supplied with moisture. Where humus is in short supply, compost some straw or bracken with an activator and add to it a small quantity of poultry manure. Shoddy is also valuable and chopped seaweed. To produce an abundance of new canes, the plants need plenty of nitrogen to stimulate new growth since short, weakly canes produce small seedy fruits and the plantation will soon die out. If plenty of humus cannot be obtained, raspberries should not be grown. Just before planting, rake in 30 g (1 oz) of sulphate of potash per metre (yard) of row or use wood ash if it has been stored under cover. It is also important to plant in clean ground for it is impossible to do so later without disturbing the fibrous roots which grow out to a considerable distance. For this reason, do not cultivate too near the canes when hoeing between the rows.

Plant the canes in late autumn before hard frosts are experienced. At that time, the soil will be still warm and friable and the canes will become established before winter. Planting can take place until early spring but not if the soil is wet or sticky after snow, or if there is frost in it. It will be better to dig a trench and 'heel in' the canes, covering the roots with straw or sacking with soil on top. They will take no harm here until conditions for planting are suitable. Always purchase Certified stock passed by the Ministry of Agriculture as being free from 'mosaic', a virus disease which will cause stunted canes. Purchase the canes from a reliable source and remember that good stock will remain vigorous almost indefinitely if it is well looked after and the original cost will be the only one.

The canes are planted 46 cm (16–18 in) apart in the rows, depending upon the vigour of the variety. 'Malling Promise' shows exceptional vigour and should be spaced 50 cm (20 in) apart. It is convenient to allow plenty of room between the rows as the plants grow tall. This is about 2.75 m (5 ft) for most varieties and 2 m (6 ft) for 'Promise' and 'Norfolk Giant'.

Take care with the planting since planting too deep is the most common cause of failure. Because the canes are long when received, it is thought that they must be put well into the ground so that they will better support themselves. This is wrong, plant no more than 2 in (5 cm) deep. The same applies to loganberries and blackberries. In fact, of all soft fruits, only black currants like deeper planting.

Make the canes firm by treading and after a few days, cut back to within 30 cm (1 ft) of soil level. This will mean that there will be no fruit the first season, apart from the autumn varieties which will fruit on the new canes formed during the summer after planting.

CARE AFTER PLANTING

Early in spring, tread the plants again for they may have become loosened by hard frost and firm planting is important to the formation of new canes. Then, when the new canes are about 46 cm (18 in) high, which will be in early summer, the rows will need staking.

Strong stakes are driven well into the ground at intervals of not more than 11 m (12 yd) to which galvanized wires are fastened about 60 cm (2 ft) and 1.5 m (5 ft) above ground. The stakes should be about 2 m (6 ft) high and as the canes continue to grow all summer, tie them in to the top wire so that if winds are troublesome, the canes will not break. Space the canes out as evenly as possible and tie in with twine which is cut away when the old canes are cut out in autumn.

Another way of supporting the canes is known as the rope method. Here the canes are fastened together in arches, tied to stout stakes 2 m (6 ft) high and at intervals of about 2 m (6 ft) so that wires are not used. The canes are bent over in arches and tied to the stakes. This partly checks the flow of sap to the tops and makes for more even ripening of the fruit along the entire length of the canes. Both methods have their advantages and staking and tying is all important since badly staked plants result in damaged canes whilst making picking a more difficult task.

During early summer the plants will benefit from a mulch of decayed manure or compost. This will help to conserve moisture in the soil and suppress weeds. It should be applied right up to the plants and to a depth of 8–10 cm (3–4 in). A mixture of partly composted lawn mowings and peat is excellent, for it readily works down into the soil during summer. In times of drought it may be necessary to water to maintain cane growth and size of fruit when the canes are in bearing. Water liberally in the evening and spray the foliage often to guard against red spider.

Straight after fruiting, the old canes are cut out to 2.5 cm (1 in) above soil level. Too much cane should not be left as it will only encourage pests and disease. Burn the old canes. End up with the new canes spaced about 10 cm (4 in) apart along the top wire. The rows will be neat and tidy and require no further attention until early next summer.

With autumn-fruiting varieties, the canes are left until early spring and are cut back to 2.5 cm (1 in) above soil level, for it is on the same year's canes that the fruit is borne. As these varieties have to produce new canes and bear fruit at the same time, provide dressings of manure or compost in the spring before growth starts.

Raspberries are gathered just before the fruit is fully ripe, whilst the berries are firm but not hard and in no way 'mushy'. If over-ripe they will be difficult to pick as they part from the core and are easily crushed. They should be red but not crimson. If covered with sugar and placed in a refrigerator for several hours they will be in perfect condition to serve with cream or after sprinkling with red wine. Alternatively, they can be frozen. The fruits will continue to ripen after picking. It is not advisable to pick the fruit if covered with moisture during rainy weather. First allow them an hour or so to dry off.

To propagate raspberries, lift a root or two in late autumn and pull off the new canes with their fibrous roots, 'teasing' them away from the old 'stool'. Any weak or stunted canes are discarded. It is not advisable to replant in ground which has been growing raspberries before. Select a fresh place and after planting as described, cut back the canes to allow the plants to form new canes the following summer.

A word of warning. When lifting the roots for propagation, and the same may be said where planting canes purchased from a grower, never allow the roots to dry out for if they do, the plants will rarely recover. Plant or 'heel in' at once or place them in a cool room with the roots in deep boxes covered with soil, until such time as they can be planted.

VARIETIES

EARLY

'GLEN MOY' A similar season to, but more concentrated than, 'Glen Clova'. The berries have a good flavour and are suitable for all purposes. The canes are moderately vigorous and have no prickles. 'Glen Moy' is resistant to greenfly which goes a long way towards protecting it from virus attack.

'MALLING PROMISE' The first of the late Mr Norman Grubb's introduction from East Malling which revolutionized raspberry growing after the war. It is the first to ripen its fruit but is more liable to frost damage than others, whilst its tall canes may also be harmed by hard frosts in winter. Best grown in the warmer parts of Britain where it has no peer, being resistant to virus and propagating well.

'GLEN CLOVA' A Scottish variety of merit, flowering late and so escaping the frosts. It bears large crops of bright red fruits which are sweet and juicy and retain their qualities after freezing.

MIDSEASON

'DELIGHT' The largest fruiting and one of the heaviest cropping varieties.

Tender-skinned so easily damaged. Of moderate flavour and really only suitable for dessert use. A vigorous grower which will produce heavy crops in its second year.

'MALLING JEWEL' The best early-mid-season variety for frost troubled gardens for its blossom opens later than others. It bears heavy crops of large, conical fruits of deep red and is excellent for freezing and bottling.

LATE

'MALLING ADMIRAL' Raised by Dr Elizabeth Keep at East Malling, it has 'Malling Promise' for one parent and possesses the same vigour, whilst it is resistant to virus and botrytis. A heavy cropper, it is one of the latest to ripen, extending the season until the autumn-fruiting varieties are ready.

'NORFOLK GIANT' This blooms late and does well in the most frost troubled gardens, and it is immune to all diseases. Cropping heavily in all soils, it is the best of all for bottling, canning and deep freezing, the fruit being firm but not as sweet as others.

VERY LATE

'LEO' So late is 'Leo' that it often doesn't start cropping until 'Delight' has finished. However, it carries on into late summer and, thus, catches the earliest of the autumn-fruiting ones. It largely replaces 'Norfolk Giant'. Moderately prickly. Good flavour and useful, if not exceptional, yields.

AUTUMN-FRUITING

'FALLGOLD' A new American variety of vigorous habit and bearing until late autumn, large yellow berries of outstanding flavour.

'ZEVA' A Swiss introduction, this is a hardy variety and makes plenty of new canes on which it begins to fruit in late summer, continuing until mid autumn. The fruits are large, almost like red blackberries and ripen to deep scarlet. They are sweet and juicy.

'AUTUMN BLISS' The newest of this type of raspberry and bred at East Malling Research Station in Kent. Its season is from late summer to early autumn and it far outyields older varieties, almost equalling that of summer varieties. Good flavour. The canes are short and sturdy and need the minimum of support.

'Glen Clova'. The popular early, summer-fruiting raspberry. Reliable, heavy cropping and resistant to several virus diseases.

CHAPTER 4

GOOSEBERRIES

This is a fruit that is at its best in a cold climate where the slow ripening brings out its subtle flavour. It does better than any fruit in the north, where it has been grown in almost every garden since the friendly rivalry of the gooseberry shows began about the year of Waterloo and made it the most popular of all fruits. It is rarely troubled by frost and is never spoilt by rain, moisture falling off the glossy skins like water off a duck's back. The fruits will hang on the bushes for several weeks and so may be used when slightly under ripe for culinary purposes and when fully ripe for dessert, when it makes as delicious eating as the best strawberries. What is more, the fruits may be picked when the weather or one's time permits and with little fear of them being over-ripe. They also bottle and freeze well. Yet so few of the hundred or so varieties in cultivation are known to modern gardeners and we miss much. Most people only know 'Careless', so much used by the canners while others, such as the olive-skinned 'Broom Girl' which bears fruit almost of golf ball size and is sweet and juicy, are completely ignored.

For an exposed garden, high above sea level, the gooseberry crops well whilst it is suitable to grow in frost hollows too. It is virtually fool-proof and rarely fails to bear heavy crops whatever the weather. By planting for succession it is possible to enjoy the fruit over several months, 'May Duke' and 'Whitesmith' being ready for culinary use at the end of spring whilst 'Leveller' and 'Howard's Lancer' will hang until mid summer and often well into late summer, 'Leveller' being much in demand at this time of year.

SOIL REQUIREMENTS

Soil is important for a good crop, gooseberries preferring a light, well drained soil but one which is well supplied with humus although an excess of nitrogenous manure is to be avoided for it encourages mildew. Work in some garden compost or small quantities of farmyard manure. Humus is necessary to conserve moisture in summer whilst the fruit is swelling and is particularly necessary for dessert varieties which will grow to a considerable size before they are at their best, when they will be sweet and juicy. Culinary varieties do not grow so large nor are they required to do so. The more nitrogen there is in the soil, the cooler will be the roots. For this reason it is most important to add large amounts of humus where growing in a shallow soil, especially over a chalk subsoil.

The plants require only sufficient nitrogen to promote the growth of new wood which may eventually take the place of older wood when the plants have grown big. Those of spreading habit will cover at least a square metre of ground; those of more upright growth will cover about half that area. Gooseberries crop both on the old and new wood, hence a three-year-old plant will bear several pounds of fruit and the quantity will increase each year.

Gooseberries are also potash lovers and as much as 28 g (2 oz) per plant of sulphate of potash should be given each year in mid spring, as a top dressing. This will enable the plants to grow 'hard' so that they will not be troubled with mildew. It will also improve the quality and flavour of the fruit. Where growing in a heavy loam, only half the amount of potash is required as for light land. It may be given in the form of wood ash stored dry. The potash content is quickly washed down to the roots by rain.

Because gooseberries resent root disturbance and send out their fibrous roots to some distance from the plant, it is essential to plant in clean ground. Where weeds compete with the gooseberries, the quality of the fruit is always poor. Nor is it advisable to hoe too near the plants in case the roots become damaged. A distance of 36 cm (15 in) from the main stem or leg must be allowed and here, a mulch of peat or garden compost will suppress weeds.

During dry weather, water copiously and to increase the size and quality of dessert varieties, water with liquid manure every ten days, preferably during showery weather. If the soil around the plants is allowed to dry out when the fruits are swelling and water is then given, it will result in split berries. So keep the hose going on the plants to prevent the roots from drying out. Gooseberries respond to watering and feeding more than any other soft fruit.

Where top quality dessert fruit is required, cut back all wood to about two-thirds of its growth each winter or to about 7.5 cm (3 in) of the new season's wood. This will direct the energies of the plant to bearing large fruits rather than to the formation of an extension to the shoots. If growing as cordons, and this is an economical way of growing gooseberries, fastening them to strong wires as for cordon apples, prune or pinch back the shoots to within 7–10 cm (3–4 in) of their base. This is best done during early spring, or in severe winters in mid spring.

For culinary varieties e.g. 'Careless', the only pruning necessary is to

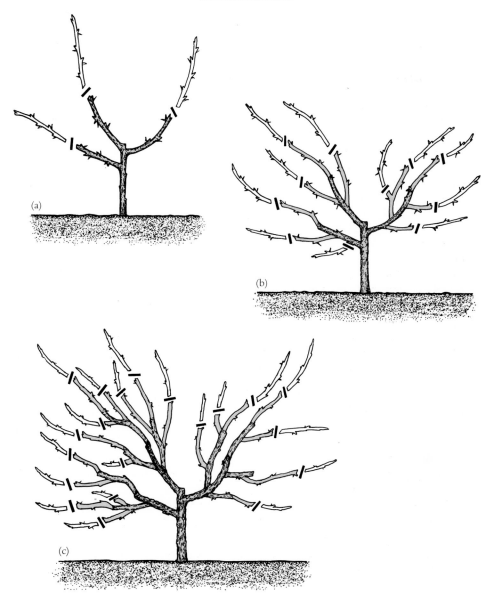

Fig. 3 (*a*) After planting a gooseberry bush (preferably a two-year-old), choose three strong shoots and prune each back by half. (*b*) The next winter, shorten the shoots retained for branches by half and all others to about 5 cm (2 in). (*c*) Continue as (*b*) until the bush is large enough, then shorten all new shoots to 2.5–5 cm (1–2 in).

cut out dead wood as it forms, which will not be until the plants are 5–6 years old.

PRUNING

Where pruning those varieties of drooping habit such as 'Whinham's Industry', cut back to an upward pointing bud to counteract this tendency, whilst those of upright habit are cut back to an outward pointing bud to prevent overcrowding at the centre. Study each variety and prune accordingly.

If growing for show or if it is desired to have dessert gooseberries of some size, it may be necessary to thin the small fruits where there is overcrowding. 'London', 'Lord Derby' and 'Princess Royal' are varieties which respond to thinning by growing to almost golf ball size. Use the thinnings for culinary purposes.

Gooseberries are grown on a 'leg' to prevent the formation of suckers. If raising plants from cuttings, use only new wood (light in colour). In late autumn remove as many shoots as you want and shorten to about 23 cm (9 in) long. Remove all but the top three buds so that the plant will have a good 'leg' and treat the severed end with hormone powder to encourage rooting. It is also important to insert them in the rooting medium, which may be a mixture of sand and peat, as quickly as possible, whilst the sap is still in the cuttings and they are moist. If allowed to become dry, they will never root.

The method is to dig a V-shaped trench 15 cm (6 in) deep and to fill it with peat and sand into which the cuttings are inserted 8–10 cm (3–4 in) apart and made firm. Early autumn is the most suitable time and, if the weather is dry, water the cuttings in and whenever the compost shows signs of drying out. If a continuous cloche of polythene sheeting is placed over the trench and closed at both ends, the moist, humid atmosphere will ensure more rapid rooting.

A single cordon is obtained by cutting back lateral shoots to a single bud and growing on the extension shoot until the plant is about 1.20 m (4 ft) tall. Cordons are grown against wires which may be fixed along the side of a path where they will take up little room. They are planted at an oblique angle to restrict the flow of sap. New growth formed during summer should be pinched back to within 5 cm (2 in) of the main stem in late summer.

A double cordon is more economical and is made by cutting back the main stem to two buds about 20 cm (8 in) above soil level, each of which face in opposite directions. From the buds, shoots are formed which are first tied to the wires at an angle of 45°, then horizontally. When the

Gooseberries are one of the best fruits for gardens. They crop regularly and heavily and may be used for cooking or dessert.

shoots have grown about 30 cm (1 ft), they are cut back to an upwards bud and grown on in vertical fashion to whatever height is desired, at the end of summer pinching back the newly formed growth on each shoot to about 5 cm (2 in) of the main stems as for single cordons. Red currants may be grown in the same way and they are also grown on a 'leg'.

Gooseberries may be planted at any time during winter, though late autumn is the most suitable time since the plants will have become established before the frosts. Planting distances will depend upon variety, those of upright habit being spaced 1.20 m (4 ft) apart; those of spreading habit 1.5–2 m (5–6 ft) apart each way. Some varieties never make large plants, 'Bedford Red' and 'Langley Gage' retain their compact habit and are ideal for the small garden, whilst 'Lancashire Lad' and 'Crown Bob' make large spreading bushes and crop heavily.

Since gooseberries tolerate partial shade, they may be planted between young orchard trees or between rows of raspberries, and strawberries may be grown for several years between the gooseberries until the gooseberries grow too large. Requiring a similar balanced diet of nitrogen and potash, these soft fruits are best grown together. The gooseberries will also provide the strawberries with protection against frost and cold winds for they come early into leaf.

Single cordons are planted 30 cm (1 ft) apart and double cordons twice that distance.

Cuttings rooted over winter should be lifted with care so as not to damage the roots and may be planted into their fruiting quarters in mid spring. If they have not by then formed roots, allow them to remain in the trenches until early autumn when they may then be moved. They will take two more years to fruit but strawberries may be planted between the rows and to within 30 cm (12 in) of the gooseberries so that the ground will be cropped to advantage. The young gooseberries will respond to a mulch each year after moving to their fruiting quarters, and keep them growing during dry weather by regular waterings. Well looked after, gooseberries will bear heavy crops for many years and require the minimum attention with their pruning.

Gooseberries ripen yellow, green, white or red, the earliest in late spring, the latest in late summer.

VARIETIES

EARLY

'BEDFORD RED' This makes a plant of neat, upright habit and is ideal for small gardens. The fruit is large and round, ripening to deep crimson.

'BROOM GIRL' Handsome and of outstanding flavour, the large round fruits ripen to deep yellow with green shading. It crops well in all soils.

'EARLY SULPHUR' Making a large spreading bush, this bears heavy crops of pale yellow fruits of outstanding flavour.

'KEEPSAKE' Almost as early as 'May Duke', this makes a large, spreading plant and crops heavily, the white, oval fruits being tinted with green and of excellent flavour.

'LANGLEY GAGE' This outstanding variety received an Award of Merit for its flavour. It makes a neat, upright bush and bears heavy crops of small, white, transparent fruits which are sweet and juicy.

'MAY DUKE' Makes a compact bush and is the earliest variety, ready to pick green in late spring to use in the kitchen; delicious for dessert in early summer by which time the fruits have turned deep red.

'WHITESMITH' Very early, this is possibly the best all-round gooseberry, bearing large, white, downy fruits along the whole length of the stems: does well in all soils.

MID-SEASON

'CARELESS' This is grown in larger numbers than any variety for it is reliable in all soils and bears heavily, the white and oval fruits being excellent for bottling, freezing and all culinary purposes.

'GUNNER' A late mid-season, ripening just before the late varieties. One of the best varieties, the olive-green berries are large and of excellent flavour.

'LAXTON'S AMBER' Making a neat upright bush, this bears heavy crops of medium-sized, amber-coloured fruits which are sweet and juicy.

'LEVELLER' The Cox's Orange of the gooseberry world, for it crops well only in Sussex and Hampshire and parts of East Anglia where the soil is to its liking. There it bears heavily, the huge, yellow berries having exceptional flavour. Of spreading habit, it is late mid-season variety.

'INVICTA' A new second-early culinary variety that is ready for picking in early summer in the south, just ahead of 'Careless'. It has the enormous benefit of being highly resistant to mildew after its early years. A very strong grower with large thorns that needs to be planted 2 m (6 ft) apart. Very heavy cropping.

'GREENFINCH' Such a new culinary variety (1987) that bushes are hard to come by. The bushes are similar in size and shape to 'Careless' but highly resistant to mildew and leaf spot. Crops more heavily then 'Careless' but with slightly smaller fruits.

LATE

'HOWARD'S LANCER' The latest of all to ripen, many people believe this

to be the best variety ever raised. A strong grower in all soils, it bears heavy crops of large, green berries which are excellent for bottling and freezing.

'LANCASHIRE LAD' This makes a big, spreading bush and bears a large, red berry when ripe, ideal for dessert; for culinary purposes picked in early summer it is still green.

'WHINHAM'S INDUSTRY' Making a big spreading plant, this ripens its crimson fruits at the same time as 'Leveller' and they may be used for dessert or culinary purposes.

'WHITE LION' The best white to mature late when it is the equal of 'Leveller' in size and flavour, whilst it bears a heavy crop in all soils.

Opposite: Black currant 'Ben Sarek'. A new variety ideal for gardens. The bushes are compact but crops are heavy and reliable.

CHAPTER 5

BLACK AND RED CURRANTS

Red and black currants require the opposite conditions to gooseberries and are more exacting in their needs. Whereas gooseberries are at their best in the cold, moist climate of the midlands and north, being frost hardy and tolerant of cold winds, black currants prefer the warmth of the south where most are grown commercially. The popularity of the black currant rests largely on its culinary value, for making pies and tarts and for preserves. Several varieties, e.g. 'Jet', which greatly extend the cropping season have removed much of the uncertainty from this crop. Even so, with the plants dropping their fruit buds in cold windy weather, black currants should not be widely planted in the north. If they are to be grown, plant those which mature late and are more tolerant of frost and cold winds, the most reliable being the 'Jet' and 'Ben Lomond'. The varieties 'Baldwin', 'Westwick Choice' and 'Boskoop Giant' should be grown only in the south for 'bud burst' is early.

Select as sheltered a position as possible for the plants and, if cold winds are troublesome, plant near a 'hedge' of hardy blackberries, where the shoots are trained along wires. Whereas gooseberries are happy in partial shade, black and red currants require an open, sunny situation, more so than any soft fruit. Black currants will remain productive for fifteen years or more.

BLACK CURRANTS

Black currants are not grown on a leg, though red currants are. With black currants, the stems or shoots are produced from buds which are below soil level and the fruit is borne along their whole length. It is important to guard against damaging the underground buds by not hoeing too near the plants. It is also necessary to encourage the formation of as much new wood as possible each year and black currants need a long growing season which is not possible in the north. They also need a soil containing plenty of moisture-holding humus and nitrogenous manures for it is nitrogen which encourages plant growth. Black currants always do better in heavy soils as long as they are well drained. Only

'Baldwin' does well on light land and perhaps 'Mendip Cross' which is of 'Baldwin' parentage; also 'Blacksmith'. Other varieties are not so fussy with regard to soil.

The plants are deep rooting in their search for food and moisture so incorporate as much humus as possible to a depth of at least 50 cm (20 in). Old mushroom-bed compost, farmyard manure and garden compost are suitable for they have a valuable nitrogen content. Hop manure (used hops from a brewery) are useful for opening up a heavy soil whilst they add 'body' to light land, soaking up and retaining moisture in summer. Straw composted with an activator and containing poultry manure, or manure from a pigeon loft will also grow good crops. Heavy land will also be opened up by incorporating some grit or old mortar and clearings from ditches which should be added to the lower 'spit' when the soil is turned over. Those near the coast will find that chopped seaweed augmented by fish meal or fish waste will supply valuable plant foods and if these are in short supply, give each plant a handful of bone meal scattered over the roots at planting time. Poultry keepers should work in feathers which are a valuable source of nitrogen; so, too, is hoof and horn meal. These are all organic manures, rich in nitrogen and they are so much better than inorganic fertilizers for black currants which never do well in a soil lacking in humus however rich it is in nitrogen. Humus is vital to conserve moisture in summer without which the plants cannot make new wood whilst the fruit will be small and seedy. Because of this, they need a mulch of peat and strawy manure or garden compost placed around each plant in late spring. This will also suppress weeds around the plant for cultivations should not be nearer than 46 cm (18 in). The surface roots will reach out to at least this distance.

Where humus is present in quantity, the plants will benefit from a 28 g per sq. m (1 oz per sq. yd) dressing of nitro-chalk given in mid spring during showery weather and again in early autumn after old wood is cut out and burnt.

Unlike gooseberries, potash is not required in quantity but if any bonfire ash is applied to the top soil at planting time, this should provide all the potash necessary.

Planting may be done at any time between late autumn and early spring but if the land is not well drained, planting in early spring is preferable. Distance apart will depend upon variety. For a small garden, for succession, plant 'Mendip Cross', 'Seabrook's' (or 'Westwick Triumph') and 'Amos Black', the latter being the latest of all, ripening its fruit in early autumn. Each of these, along with modern varieties, is of compact habit and may be planted 1.2–1.5 m (4–5 ft) apart without overcrowding. Those of vigorous habit like 'Westwick Choice' and 'Wellington XXX' should be allowed an extra 46 cm (18 in) both in and between the rows. The compact variety 'Ben Sarek' need only be 1.2 m (4 ft) apart. More economic use of the ground can be made by planting slightly closer in the rows and with greater spacing between the rows so that a double row of strawberries can be planted between. By planting closer in the rows, damage by frost and cold winds is less likely. Be sure that the ground is clear of weeds before planting for to cultivate too near the plants afterwards will be to greatly reduce the crop if the underground buds are damaged.

Black currants are planted about 15 cm (6 in) deep, which is deeper than most soft fruits, and trodden in firmly. Plant when the soil is friable and contains no frost.

CARE AFTER PLANTING

In early spring, cut back all wood to about 7–8 cm (3 in) of soil level. This will stimulate the underground buds into growth and a bushy plant will be quickly built up. At the same time tread in any plants lifted from the ground by frost.

It should be said that only reliable plants from a good grower should be obtained, guaranteed free from big bud or reversion, a virus disease caused by the gall mite when the flower buds fail to open and little fruit is obtained. Reliable growers supply 'guaranteed' stock at no extra cost. A two-year-old bush is the best to plant.

Pruning of established plants (and they will bear no fruit the first year) will not be necessary until they have been growing for at least three years. Afterwards, cut out any dead wood or, where there is overcrowding, almost to the base. Also, any unduly long shoots may be cut back to a 'break' bud and the newly formed shoot grown on. This will prevent the older plants from forming too much old wood and so keep them vigorous and healthy.

The best way of preventing a build-up of old wood is to prune back to its point of origin any branch that is four years old. Branches of this age will fruit poorly and will produce very few new shoots.

Black currants are the easiest of soft fruits to propagate. In early

Opposite: Red currant 'Red Lake'. A popular garden variety with large juicy berries. Reliable and free-cropping; moderately vigorous bush.

autumn, after fruiting has ended, cut out a shoot or two of the new season's wood from each plant. Shorten these to some 23 cm (9 in) in length and insert them in trenches of peat and sand so that only the top 5–8 cm (2–3 in) is showing. Roots will start to form in the spring but allow them to grow on during summer and in autumn plant them in their final positions and cut back all shoots to 7–8 cm (3 in) to build up a bushy plant for the following year. The following year they will come into fruit. Regular spraying with a systemic fungicide will keep the plants free from rust and leaf spot (see Chapter 9).

VARIETIES

A great deal of breeding work has been put into black currants in recent years which has resulted in many of the older varieties becoming redundant. The main advance has been in the later flowering, which avoids damage to the plants by spring frosts.

EARLY
'MENDIP CROSS' Raised from 'Boskoop Giant', this possesses all its good qualities and none of its defects. Making a compact bush, it is resistant to frost and cold winds whilst it bears heavy crops of sweet, juicy fruit.

MID-SEASON
'BLACKSMITH' Bud burst is late so this variety may be planted to follow 'Wellington XXX' in frosty areas. It is a reliable and heavy cropper even in light soils, the fruit being borne in long double trusses.
'TENAH' A new Dutch variety which is tolerant of frost and cold winds and bears heavy crops of medium-sized fruits.
'WESTWICK TRIUMPH' Of compact habit, bud burst is so late that it may be grown with every chance of heavy crops in those gardens troubled by late frosts. As an additional bonus, the fruit is large and sweet and borne in very long trusses.

LATE
'AMOS BLACK' Making a plant of slender upright habit, this is a good late for a small garden, being the last to ripen its fruit and flowering late it misses all frosts. It bears a heavy crop of medium-sized, thick-skinned fruits.
'COTSWOLD CROSS' Of the same parentage as 'Amos Black', this is equally good, cropping well in all districts and in all soils and bearing its large, juicy berries in short compact clusters.

NEW VARIETIES

The new generation of black currants is far superior to the traditional varieties. They crop more heavily, most are resistant to mildew and they are better able to cope with spring frosts.

'BEN LOMOND' The main commercial variety nowadays that has taken over from 'Baldwin', which used to be the most widely grown variety. Mid-season with its fruits ripening in mid summer. The large berries are suitable for all purposes but the flavour is slightly weaker than older varieties. It is late flowering, up to two weeks after 'Baldwin', and has a good resistance to cold weather.

'BEN MORE' 7–10 days earlier than 'Ben Lomond'. Very late flowering, sometimes three weeks later than 'Baldwin', and resistant to frosts but does not crop very heavily. Low vitamin C content. Vigorous and upright growth.

'BEN NEVIS' The bushes are larger than 'Ben Lomond' but the crop soon bends down the branches. It flowers about a week after 'Baldwin' and, thus, is less likely to be frosted. Lower yields than 'Ben Lomond' but heavier than 'Baldwin'.

'BEN SAREK' Likely to become the best garden variety because the bushes are considerably smaller than others and yet yields are as great. Flowers at the same time as 'Baldwin' but has some resistance to cold and frost. Crops heavily with larger than average berries.

'MALLING JET' A strong growing and slightly spreading variety that holds up well under the weight of it's crop. Late flowering and correspondingly late fruiting. Heavy cropping. Very seldom caught by spring frosts. It has long fruit clusters which make it easy to pick. Ripe fruit will stay on the bush for some time without spoiling.

RED CURRANTS

At one time grown for its ability to set jam the red currant has, since the extraction of pectin from apples, become less common and is now seen in few gardens, yet for conserves to accompany meats and for pies, few fruits can match it. Growing on a 'leg', like gooseberries, it is not so heavy cropping, whilst the scarlet fruits attract birds so that plants should be netted when the fruit begins to ripen. Against this, the plants will crop for many years and are less troubled by pest and disease than any other fruit.

Red currants enjoy the same soil conditions as the gooseberry and are often grown with them, planting one here and there in the rows. A light, deeply dug soil containing plenty of humus rather than nitrogenous manures suits it best and though it prefers light land, humus is necessary to retain summer moisture without which the fruits remain small and seedy. But with ample moisture they swell as large as black currants and are sweet and juicy.

At planting time, rake in 28 g (1 oz) of sulphate of potash to each plant or plenty of wood ash which has been stored under cover and repeat this in mid spring each year. The plants also appreciate a summer mulch of decayed manure or garden compost given in early summer.

Planting is done late autumn – early winter before hard frosts, setting the plants about 1.20 m (4 ft) apart. Before planting, remove any roots which may have formed up the stem or 'leg' and which might cause suckers to form if left on.

Select a position sheltered from cold winds. They are best planted among gooseberries for protection. For this reason, red currants usually crop better in the south. Plant firmly.

The minimum of pruning is necessary for, like gooseberries, the fruit is borne both on the old and new wood. New shoots are cut back to within 7–8 cm (3 in) of their base to encourage fruit buds and to ensure good-sized berries. This is done early in spring so that the energy of the plant will be directed to the formation of good fruit whilst at the same time, a compact head will be built up. In later years, any dead wood must be cut out.

Red currants may also be grown (like gooseberries) as single or double cordons in the manner described for gooseberries. In this way, they may be grown against a sunny wall or alongside a path provided they are sheltered from cold winds. Also, they must be in the open, in full sun. They never do well in semi-shade. Single cordons are planted 50 cm (20 in) apart, at an oblique angle and tied in to wires; double cordons are planted 60 cm (2 ft) apart, and here the shoots on either side the 'leg' are grown upright. Small pieces of tin fastened to the wires so that they jingle in the breeze will help to scare off the birds.

To propagate, remove 30 cm (12 in) long shoots of the new season's wood about mid autumn and after removing all except the upper three buds, treat the base with hormone powder to encourage rooting and plant in a V-trench containing peat and sand. The shoots will take a year to root, after which they are moved to their fruiting quarters. They will come into fruit the following year.

Opposite: These heavy cropping, dwarf Cox trees illustrate that there is room in every garden for at least one apple tree.

VARIETIES

EARLY
'JONKHEER VAN TETS' A new Dutch variety making a large plant and cropping heavily, its large, crimson fruits being sweet and juicy.
'LAXTON'S NO. 1' A strong grower and reliable cropper in all districts, this is the first to mature, the fruits being of rich red though not so large as those of 'Red Lake' which follows it. It does well in all soils.

MID-SEASON
'RED LAKE' Raised in Minnesota, U.S.A., it is, with 'Laxton's No. 1', the most reliable variety for all soils and all districts whilst the berries are of dessert size, being almost as large as black currant and sweet and juicy. The fruit is borne in long trusses.
'STANZA' (Dutch) A new late mid season variety normally making a small and compact bush. Flowers two weeks later than 'Red Lake' but fruits only a few days later. High yielding.

LATE
'REDSTART' A very new, late variety cropping at least half as much again as 'Red Lake'. It flowers a week later than 'Red Lake' and fruits 1–2 weeks later. The small to medium-sized fruits are produced on long clusters. They are bright red with a good acid flavour. It makes good jelly and is likely to replace the late variety 'Rondom'.

WHITE CURRANTS

This is simply a colourless variety of the red currant, therefore its cultivation is exactly the same. The main variety is 'White Versailles' but the later flowering 'White Transparent' is useful where spring frosts are troublesome.

CHAPTER 6

BLACKBERRIES AND HYBRID BERRIES

These are the last of the soft fruits in the season, ripening throughout autumn and extending the season until late autumn. They are also the hardiest, being in no way troubled by frost and cold winds. Indeed, they may be planted as a wind break, along the side of the garden where the prevailing wind is most felt and here they act as protection for other soft fruits. Blackberries and many hybrid berries which are of blackberry or loganberry parentage freeze well so that there is no waste with the crop, whilst the introduction of thornless varieties is giving them a new popularity.

They may be planted against a sunless wall where few other fruits will grow well, tying in the long arching shoots or canes to trellis or wires. They may be used to cover trellis or rustic fencing which may have been erected to divide one part of the garden from another or to hide a corner where dustbins are kept, whilst 'Himalaya Giant', with its large thorns, may be used for an outer hedge, training the shoots along wires fastened to strong posts driven well into the ground. In two years, the plants will have formed a hedge which when 1.50 m (5 ft) high will be impenetrable, whilst the weight of fruit will be enormous. They may be planted in this way along the side of the garden against prevailing winds where they will crop heavily. Loganberries, with their brittle wood are not suitable for this purpose and crop better in the more sheltered gardens of the south and west. They are also less hardy.

The hybrid berries are also planted in rows, allowing 1.50 m (5 ft) between each row and planting 4.5 m (12–15 ft) apart for the more vigorous varieties and 3–4 m (10–12 ft) for those of less vigour. Where possible, plant thornless varieties for the work of tying in the shoots is less tedious and damaging to the hands. Against this, they crop less heavily than thorny ones.

Another way to grow them is against poles which stand about 2 m (6–7 ft) above ground, with about 1 m (3 ft) buried in the ground. In this way blackberries may be planted between rows of gooseberries and loganberries with black currants, for the shoots are grown perpendicular and tied to the poles like climbing roses. About every third year, the shoots are untied and allowed to fall to the ground when all wood that has fruited is cut out before the shoots are tied in again. If loganberries are grown in this way, the old wood is removed each year in late autumn for they fruit only on the new season's wood. Blackberries and those hybrid berries of blackberry parentage crop both on the old and new wood, hence bear prolifically but the plants will be kept healthier and will bear heavier crops if kept free of too much old wood.

SOIL REQUIREMENTS

Loganberries and the other hybrids require large amounts of nitrogenous manures to help them produce an abundance of new cane growth each year. This is given as farmyard manure, poultry manure or garden compost. Humus is necessary to maintain moisture in the soil during summer when the plants are making new growth. Blackberries do not need to make so much new wood, sufficient only to maintain a balance between the old and the new, so that the plants remain healthy and vigorous. Work in whatever organic manures are available and each year give all plants a heavy mulch of garden compost in late spring.

Before mulching, give each plant 28 g (1 oz) of sulphate of potash which is raked into the surface. This is given in mid spring during showery weather. It will improve the quality of fruit and build up a hard plant, better able to withstand cold winds.

Mulching is important and in a dry summer will enable the plants to produce an extra pound or two of fruit each and, at the same time, plenty of new wood. Blackberries form many of their roots just below the surface of the soil and, if shaded from the sun by the mulch which will also keep them moist, the plants will respond by remaining healthy and vigorous for thirty years or more. Lawn mowings are better used for mulching when partly composted. If not, and they are applied thickly, they may heat up and damage the surface roots. The use of a mulch will almost do away with the need to water the plants, though they will appreciate an occasional spraying in hot dry weather, whilst watering with diluted liquid manure every fortnight will increase the weight and quality of the fruit.

Take care not to take the hoe too near the plants for they send out their surface roots to at least 60 cm (2 ft). Rely on mulching close to the plants to suppress weeds.

The time to prepare the ground and to plant is late autumn – early winter, usually before hard frost and the plants will be settled in before they begin to make new growth early in spring. Planting, however, may take place whenever the ground is free of frosts, until early spring.

PRUNING

Blackberries and the hybrid berries resent deep planting. Plant only just beneath the surface so that the roots are just covered but make firm by treading in. The posts, or the poles against which the plants will grow, should have been creosoted where they will be below soil level and should be in position before planting so that the roots are not disturbed. Between the posts, wires are fixed 90, 120, 150 and 180 cm (3, 4, 5 and 6 ft) above the ground.

After planting, cut back the stems to within 15 cm (6 in) of soil level to stimulate the plants to form new wood during their first year, tying in the shoots as they form. Blackberries, tayberries, and sunberries are tied to the wires horizontally, but loganberries which are of more raspberry habit and produce their arching stems (canes) almost upright, are tied to the wires fan-like rather than horizontally for if any attempt is made to bend them unduly, they will snap.

Loganberries also require the same pruning as raspberries, cutting out the old shoots in late autumn, after fruiting, to the base. The new shoots are tied in as they form during summer. The loganberry fruits at the same time as the raspberry, being the first of the hybrid berries to do so. It will crop until late summer when the first blackberries are ripe.

To propagate blackberries and the hybrid berries of blackberry parentage, simply bend over one or two young shoots from each plant and in late summer, bury the tips in the soil to which a little peat is incorporated. Tread firmly and keep the soil moist. By late autumn, roots will have formed at the tips when they are severed from the parent but left in position until early spring when they are lifted and replanted where they are to fruit. Loganberries can also be propagated by lifting a root or two and pulling away the canes as for raspberries.

VARIETIES OF BLACKBERRY

'BEDFORD GIANT' The first of the blackberries to ripen in late summer and excellent for freezing. It crops well under all conditions, the large firm fruits being sweet and juicy.

'ASHTON CROSS' This ripens its fruit after 'Bedford Giant' and before 'Himalaya Giant' and is a vigorous grower, highly resistant to virus. In good soil it crops heavily, the large round berries being of good flavour. A selection of the wild blackberry.

'HIMALAYA GIANT' This variety possesses extreme hardiness and crops heavily both on the old and new wood. Since its introduction in 1900, it has been widely planted as a hedge or wind break but its large thorns make picking difficult. The fruit is large and firm so that it bottles and freezes well.

'OREGON THORNLESS' Likely to supersede all others for mid-season for its fern-like foliage is most handsome, whilst an established plant will yield 4.5–5.5 kg (10–12 lb) of large juicy berries between early and mid autumn. What is more, it is thornless, making picking and tying a pleasure. Is now grown instead of the lighter cropping 'Merton Thornless'.

VARIETIES OF HYBRID BERRY

'BOYSENBERRY' Of American origin and said to be a cross between a loganberry and blackberry with the habit and flavour of the former. A plant of vigorous habit the large mulberry-red fruits ripen through early autumn. Only really hardy in the south of the U.K.

'JAPANESE WINEBERRY' A handsome plant, introduced from the East a century ago and perfectly hardy. The soft green leaves are white on the underside whilst the canes are covered with crimson hairs rather than thorns. Could be grown as an ornamental climber. In late summer it bears masses of golden fruits of raspberry size and of unusual, grape-like flavour.

'LOGANBERRY' Believed to be a seedling from an open-pollinated wild dewberry, *Rubus ursinus,* this bears a long tapering crimson fruit which does not part from its 'plug' and so retains its shape after bottling and freezing. It must be fully ripe before using. It fruits only on the new wood and since the canes are often troubled by frost and cold winds, it should only be grown south of the Trent. It ripens its fruit during mid to late summer. The new thornless variety LY654 is better in every way, being of more vigorous habit and a pleasure to pick. The best thorny selection is LY59.

'YOUNGBERRY' A loganberry–blackberry cross and like all those hybrids of this parentage, crops and grows better in a warm garden. The berries ripen purple-black with the loganberry flavour whilst as many as 4.5 kg (10 lb) of fruit may be picked from a single plant. It crops from late summer to early autumn. There is now a thornless variety which makes for easier picking.

'SUNBERRY' A blackberry × raspberry hybrid raised at East Malling Research Station and released for general use in 1981. The vigorous and spiny canes produce large crops of loganberry-type fruits which are glossy and almost black. Their season is from mid to late summer. In trials, the cumulative crop over a five-year period was 43.5 kg (96 lb) per plant compared with 23 kg (50 lb) for LY654 and 22 kg (48 lb) for tay-berry. Their cultivation is the same as for loganberries except the plants should be 5 m (15 ft) apart.

'TAYBERRY' A cross between the American blackberry 'Aurora' and an un-named raspberry seedling. Its season starts at the same time as the sunberry but continues beyond it into late summer. Less acid and better flavoured than loganberries and also hardier. Moderately vigorous and prickly.

CHAPTER 7

APPLES AND PEARS

Apples and pears are the most widely grown of the top, or tree, fruits, apples being hardier and better able to set good crops in the north and in gardens exposed to cold winds than pears, which prefer the warmth of the south. The apple is native of Europe including Britain, the pear of Southern Europe: in France and Italy it grows to perfection, but here it should be given the warmest part of the garden. Apples can be planted in less favourable places. Flowering later, they are less likely to be caught by spring frosts.

APPLES

Apples grow best in a loamy soil that is well drained. Most difficult are those soils of a limestone nature where there is little depth of top soil. The result is that in a dry year, there is not sufficient moisture for the fruit to grow large and juicy. Such a soil may be made more fertile by adding quantities of decayed manure or garden compost, digging it in as deeply as possible.

APPLES FOR DIFFICULT SOILS

The only soils that apples really dislike are shallow ones overlying chalk or, to a lesser extent, limestone. These not only tend to dry out in the summer but they can also give rise to what is called a 'lime-induced deficiency' in some of the essential food elements, notably iron, purely on account of them being strongly alkaline.

Where this occurs, the leaves are pale or even yellow and crops will suffer considerably.

The simplest way to overcome the problem is to reduce the alkalinity by adding an acidic material to the soil at planting time. The normal one is peat. This is strongly acid and will counteract the alkalinity to the point at which all elements are again available to the tree.

It is also desirable, though normally only in the early years, to treat the ground around the base of the tree each spring with sequestrene. This is

Not every home can aspire to a walled garden but smaller versions of these espalier apples can easily be accommodated.

readily available in most garden centres and shops.

A heavy, clay soil may be brought into better shape by incorporating any form of bulky organic manure such as farmyard manure, old mushroom-bed compost, or garden compost.

For clay soil, 'Adam's Pearmain' is hardy and tolerant of such a soil. Its fruit is mature in late winter. 'Newton Wonder', raised in Derbyshire, and one of the handsomest of all apples also does well on clay. 'Edward VII' is also suitable and will keep until mid spring, and, for dessert, 'James Grieve', raised in Scotland.

For wet, low-lying land, work in as much drainage material as possible and some peat and decayed manure. For such a soil, the finest dessert apple is 'Laxton's Superb', at its best in early winter. For culinary use, choose 'Grenadier', the best of all pollinators for 'Bramley's Seedling'. 'Lord Derby' also does well in wet soils.

To bring a light, sandy soil into condition, dig in plenty of humus in any form as this hold the moisture about the roots in summer. Such a soil will usually be deficient in potash so rake in some wood ash or give 28 g (1 oz) of sulphate of potash spread around each tree after planting. In light soils, for dessert, plant 'Ellison's Orange' which makes a compact tree and comes quickly into bearing; and 'Cox's Orange' with its pollinator 'Worcester Pearmain', the latter making a large tree and being tip bearing.

Planting may be done whenever the ground is in a friable condition between late autumn and early spring, the earlier the better so that the trees will become established before the frosts. Aim to plant at the same depth that the tree was at in the nursery, as shown by the soil ring just above the roots. Too shallow planting will cause the roots to dry out in a hot summer; too deep planting will mean that the roots are in the less fertile subsoil. It is important to make the hole large enough to allow the roots to be spread well out after shortening the tap root or any unduly long roots. Over them, place a spadeful of mixed sand and peat and replace the soil, treading firmly.

Rootstocks play in important part in determining planting distances. M9 and M26 produce small trees which come quickly into bearing. Both are used for cordon and pyramid trees. Plant cordons 1 m (3–4 ft) apart, pyramids 1.8 m (6 ft). MM106 rootstock is now used for virtually all bush apple trees. They should be planted 4–5 m (12–15 ft) apart, according to the vigour of the variety and the quality of the soil.

TYPES OF TREE

Spur-forming apples may be planted as cordons alongside a path where

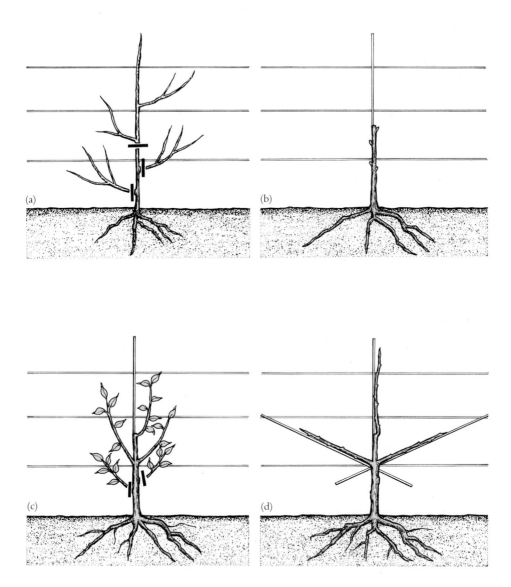

Fig. 4 Forming an espalier apple or pear. (*a*) Unless already a basic espalier, remove all side shoots after planting; shorten central stem to 1–2 buds above bottom wire. (*b*) Prune maiden trees back to 1–2 buds above the bottom support wire. (*c*) First summer after planting. Choose two shoots to form bottom pair of branches and remove any below them. (*d*) First winter. Tie in lowest pair of branches to canes; shorten central leader to 2–3 buds above second wire.

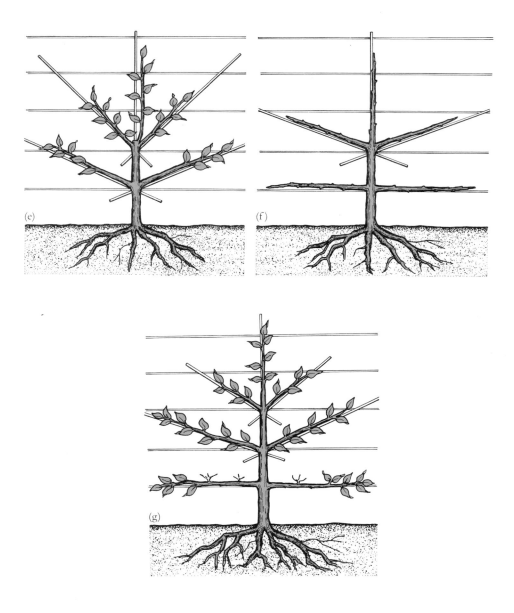

Fig. 4 (*contd.*) (*e*) Second summer. Select and retain second pair of branches and central leader. Treat as before. (*f*) Second winter. Bend second pair of branches lower and bottom pair to horizontal. Shorten central leader to 2–3 buds above third wire. (*g*) Continue as before. Any side shoots are cut back to 3–4 buds in the winter.

they take up little room. They are trained against wires and are planted at an oblique angle to limit growth. Do not plant tip bearers, such as 'Worcester Pearmain', as cordons. Maiden (one-year-old) trees are planted, allowing the leader shoot to grow on to 1.8 m (6–7 ft). In late summer, pinch back lateral shoots to 15 cm (6 in) to build up fruiting spurs as quickly as possible. They will begin to fruit in their second year after planting.

Bush trees are pruned to the open centre plan. Here, the main lateral is cut back to 75 cm (30 in). Laterals are formed below this point which will grow on to become the branches. Allow them to grow on for one year, then 'tip' them so that each stem will then form laterals and these are cut back by half each year.

The dwarf pyramid form is now popular. With this, a compact, heavy cropping tree is built up in the quickest time. After planting the maiden tree, cut the leader back to 50 cm (20 in) high. Side shoots longer than 15 cm (6 in) are shortened to about 13 cm (5 in). Next winter, cut back the new growth on the central leader to 20–25 cm (8–10 in) to a bud pointing in the opposite direction to that in which the shoot grew in the first year. Shorten all other shoots to 15–20 cm (6–8 in).

Pears are treated in the same way but may also be grown against a wall or along wires in the espalier or horizontal form. They take up little space. Here, too, maidens are planted, the leader being shortened to about 46 cm (18 in) above ground, to a point where there are two buds, one on either side of the stem. These will form the first arms or tier of the tree. As they grow, the arms are tied to the wires whilst the vertical extension shoot is allowed to grow on for another 46 cm (18 in) before it is again cut back to two opposite buds. These will form the second pair of arms and so the tree is built up to the required height, usually one tier being formed each year. If growing against the wall of a house, the tree may be grown to a height of 8–10 m (30–40 ft) and each year bear a huge crop.

When the first tier has formed, in its second season, all side growths are pinched back at the end of summer to 13 cm (5 in). This will encourage the plant to form fruiting buds instead of more new wood and it will begin to crop the following year. Fruiting will be further encouraged if the arms are also cut back to about half the new wood in early winter, making the cut to a bud which will grow on to form the new wood the following year.

If, as sometimes happens, a bud will fail to 'break', which would mean the loss of an arm or a badly balanced tree, it will be necessary to persuade the bud to 'break' by making a notch and removing the bark immediately above it.

SOIL REQUIREMENTS

Apples and pears will benefit from a mulch of strawy manure given in spring and spread around the trees. Before it is applied, give each tree a sprinkling of sulphate of potash for this will encourage the formation of fruiting spurs and will improve the quality of fruit. A balanced diet is necessary; nitrogen to make new wood, phosphates for root production and potash to encourage flowering and fruiting. If established trees are not making sufficient growth, in early spring give each a 28 g (1 oz) dressing of sulphate of ammonia, raking it into the surface. This will stimulate the trees into growth.

Apples may sometimes show signs of magnesium deficiency when the leaves turn pale green and fall before their time. If uncorrected, the trees become stunted. If observed, spray the trees in early summer with a solution of magnesium sulphate (Epsom salts), 224 g dissolved in 9 l (8 oz dissolved in 2 gal) of water when the magnesium will be absorbed through the leaves. If a handful of blood, fish and bone fertilizer is lightly forked into the soil around the trees, this contains all the plant foods and can be followed by a spring mulch of decayed manure or composted straw.

Bush trees, and any larger, will need staking, unless the garden is sheltered. Use a proper stake driven well into the ground and reaching to just beneath the head. It is better to put the stake in place before covering in the roots. For a tie, use a piece of old tyre inner tubing or one of the special rubber or plastic ties. It is important that the tree does not rub against the stake.

POLLINATION

Before ordering the trees, some thought must be given to pollination. It is no use planting a row of cordon 'Cox's Orange Pippin' and expecting to enjoy heavy crops without a suitable pollinator. With 'Cox's' it has been proved that where 'Worcester Pearmain', 'James Grieve' or 'Egremont Russet' are used for its pollination the setting of fruit is better than that obtained by using any other pollinators.

Where certain varieties are required, make sure they will pollinate each other and it is usual that varieties in bloom at the same time will do so. For example, where frosts are troublesome, it is better to plant late flowering culinary varieties such as 'Crawley Beauty' and 'Edward VII', amongst the best of all keepers and with them 'Lane's Prince Albert' which flowers over a longer season than any other apple. In a good year when there are plenty of pollinating insects about, one or two apples will set their own pollen. These include 'Rev. Wilks' (early), 'Sunset' and

'Grenadier' (mid-season) and 'Crawley Beauty' (late). They are a good selection for all purposes. However, every variety succeeds best when cross-pollinated.

When choosing pollinators, remember that several varieties are triploids and cannot pollinate others or themselves and so require to be planted with two other varieties (which are not triploids).

Although cross-pollination is essential if full crops of good-quality fruits are to be had, too much importance can be placed on the need to plant more than one variety. In all except the most isolated homes, there will almost certainly be other varieties in neighbouring or nearby gardens that will provide adequate cross-pollination. After all, bees (the main carriers of pollen) will travel considerable distances whilst collecting nectar. However, it is as well to know which varieties will and will not make good pollinators.

Pollination compatibility table:

Key

T = Triploid: sterile pollen. All others are diploids and have fertile pollen.

These flower early mid-season:

'Annie Elizabeth'   'Ellison's Orange'
'Fortune'   'Grenadier'
'Bramley's Seedling' (T)   'James Grieve'
'Kent'   'Lord Lambourne'
'Cox's Orange Pippin'   'Sunset'
'Discovery'   'Greensleeves'
'Egremont Russet'   'Worcester Pearmain'

These flower late mid-season:

'Blenheim Orange' (T)   'Lane's Prince Albert'
'Charles Ross'   'Laxton's Superb'
'Lord Derby'   'Newton Wonder'
'Spartan'   'Sunset'
'Howgate Wonder'

These bloom late:

'Fiesta'   'Edward VII'
'Bountiful'   'Jester'
'Suntan' (T)

Any planted together in each section will ensure satisfactory pollination.

'Conference' pear. The most widely grown commercial and home variety for nearly 100 years. Usually reliable with heavy crops.

Heavy crops are virtually assured when pears are grown as espaliers trained to wires. Also, they are very economical of space.

PEARS

With pears, the same rules apply though they do require greater warmth to crop well and to ripen the fruit properly. Yet there is no reason why the hardier varieties e.g. 'Jargonelle', 'Catillac' and 'Durondeau' cannot be grown in the cooler parts and also 'Gorham' and 'William's Bon Chretien' if planted against a warm wall. These pears are hardy and only bloom late but all pears bloom at least two weeks before apples and are more susceptible to frost damage. Whilst there are several apples which bear well in a limestone soil, there are few pears which grow well in such a soil. Pears require a soil containing plenty of humus for they must never lack moisture at the roots, especially where growing against a wall, so make sure that you work in plenty of decayed manure, garden compost or composted straw.

The same rules of pollination apply to pears as to apples. It is advisable to plant near each other several trees which bloom at the same time for there will be fewer pollinating insects about, especially when the first blossom appears. Those hardy pears, 'Jargonelle', 'Catillac' and 'Pitmaston Duchess' are triploids and cannot set their own blossom or that of their pollinator so plant two pollinators with any of these. And remember that the fertile 'Conference' will not pollinate 'Beurre d'Amanlis', and 'Seckle' will not pollinate 'Louise Bonne', though both bloom together.

Though a number are self-fertile, all pears will set a greater amount of fruit if grown with others in bloom at the same time.

Pear pollination compatibility table:

These pears bloom early and should be omitted from frost-troubled gardens:

'Conference'	'Durondeau'
'Beth'	'Louise Bonne'
'Packham's Triumph'	

These pears bloom mid-season:

'Beurré Superfin'	'Josephine de Malines'
'Glou Morceau'	'William's Bon Chretien'

These pears bloom late:

'Clapp's Favourite'	'Doyenne du Comice'
'Gorham'	'Winter Nelis'
'Onward'	

EARLY

'DOYENNE D'ETE' Small yellow fruits. Juicy and pleasant flavour. Crops well but tree usually weak and small.

'JARGONELLE' One of the hardiest of early pears. Useful in the north and in Scotland.

TO RIPEN EARLY AUTUMN

'BETH' A comparatively new English pear particularly recommended for gardens. Ripens to pale yellow with pink flush. Melting, juicy flesh with rich, sweet flavour.

'GORHAM' An American seedling from Williams. Hardy and less prone to scab disease.

'MERTON PRIDE' A green pear raised at the John Innes Institute in the 1940s. Very melting and juicy with strong pear flavour.

'ONWARD' A new English-bred pear. Heavy crops of large greenish fruit with an orange flush are carried from early in life. Soft, melting flesh; very juicy and sweet. Excellent garden variety.

'WILLIAM'S BON CHRETIEN' It is the Bartlett pear of the American canners and though over 200 years old, it remains one of the best early pears ever raised, cropping well everywhere, its musky flavour is renowned. It should be picked green.

TO RIPEN MID AUTUMN

'CONFERENCE' The most reliable of pears, it is a valuable pollinator for mid-season varieties and bears heavy crops, the dark green fruits being russeted when ripe.

'BEURRE HARDY' Although an excellent quality and very hardy pear, the tree is so large and vigorous that it is only suitable where there is plenty of room.

'BEURRE SUPERFIN' A high quality pear that really only gives of its best in a warm position. Juicy and melting flesh of superb flavour. Of moderate growth and cropping potential.

TO RIPEN LATE AUTUMN

'DURONDEAU' Making a compact tree of great hardiness, the fruit ripens to deep gold with a crimson cheek and will keep until late autumn.

'LOUISE BONNE' This makes a large tree and crops heavily but only in the warmth of the south-west. the green fruit has red flesh and outstanding flavour.

'PACKHAM'S TRIUMPH' A vigorous grower and free cropper, the fruit is similar in appearance and flavour to 'Comice' but is without that pear's difficulties in culture and should be planted instead.

'DOYENNE DU COMICE' Accepted by most people as being the finest flavoured dessert pear. Unreliable at cropping but good when conditions suit it. Large golden fruits with a slight russet and red flush. Best when grown against a warm wall. Late flowering so should have another late variety, e.g. 'Gorham', 'Winter Nelis' or 'Onward', close at hand. Juicy, sweet and melting flesh of highest quality.

TO RIPEN EARLY – MID WINTER

'GLOU MORCEAU' Flesh juicy and melting with excellent flavour; fairly large and yellowish when ripe. One of the finest late pears but, like others, only at it's best against a warm wall when it is reliable and quite heavy cropping.

'JOSEPHINE DE MALINES' Another excellent-quality, late, dessert pear but with a similar liking for a warm wall.

'WINTER NELIS' A medium to small pear covered with a dull russet. Good quality and keeps well. Quite fertile and free from scab.

TO RIPEN EARLY – MID SPRING

'CATILLAC' This pear blooms late, is a vigorous grower and crops well. The large, dull crimson fruits should not be harvested until late autumn and, if stored as cool as possible, will keep until mid spring. The most widely grown cooking pear.

CHAPTER 8

PEACHES, CHERRIES AND PLUMS

Peaches, cherries and plums are the most important of the stone fruits, requiring a soil containing adequate lime. They are the most reliable fruits for planting in a limestone soil They all grow a crop well in East Anglia; in Kent and Sussex; and in Hereford and Worcestershire where orchards in bloom are a familiar sight in spring.

PEACHES

Peaches require a sunny situation, sheltered from cold winds and are best grown in the fan-shape against a sunny wall. They require no manure apart from a little bone meal but lime rubble should be worked into the soil before planting.

Planting is done in late autumn, allowing 3.5–4.5 m (12–15 ft) distance apart for fan trees. Take out a hole large enough for the roots to be spread well out and, as the soil is replaced, sprinkle in it 56 g (2 oz) of bone meal for each tree. The variety will have been grafted on to 'St. Julien "A"' plum rootstocks so when planting, make sure that the union of the graft is above soil level so that it will not form roots here. Plant firmly and keep the trees well supplied with moisture during summer. Evaporation of moisture from the soil will be reduced if in late spring, the plants are given a thick mulch of decayed manure or garden compost. It is essential that the trees do not lack moisture whilst the fruits are swelling.

PRUNING

The peach bears its fruit on the previous year's wood and there will be little fruit if the wood has not been well ripened by the sun. At the end of spring, new growth formed by the leader shoots is cut back by about one-third whilst in mid-summer, the tips of the side growths are pinched out when about 8 cm (3 in) long. A single wood bud will be retained at the base of each shoot to grow on as a replacement for next year's fruit, the shoot which has borne fruit being removed at the end of the season;

Peach 'Peregrine' is the hardiest variety and can be grown to perfection when fan-trained to a sunny wall.

though during the first years of the tree, fruiting shoots are allowed to grow on until reaching 46 cm (18 in). This is fastened to wires and the tip pinched back to a wood bud and on the shoot formed here will be borne the next year's crop. Wood buds are small and pointed; blossom buds are fat and round.

Peaches must be encouraged to produce as much new wood as possible for if the old wood is not continually cut out, the plants will soon stop bearing.

Shoots appearing next to a fruit are pinched out above the second leaf and this removal of unwanted growth should be spread over the whole of early summer.

Thinning of overcrowded fruit must not be done until after 'stoning'. This is a natural falling off of fruits when they are about the size of a

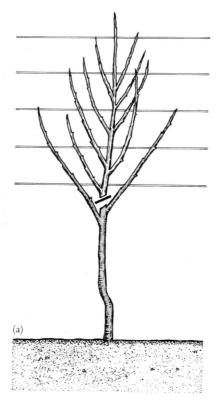

Fig. 5 Forming a fan tree. (*a*) After planting the peach tree, select two shoots for lowest main branches and remove central stem above them.

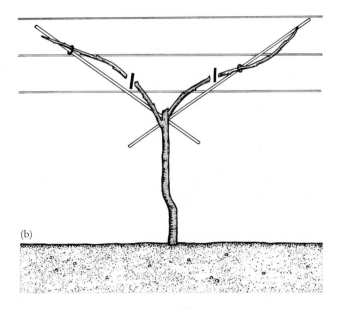

(b)

Fig. 5 (*contd.*) (*b*) Shorten back retained shoots by up to half and tie in to canes.

walnut, and it may not be necessary to remove others, though there should be about 15 cm (6 in) between each of those fruits left to mature.

The fruit is ripe when the palm of the hand is placed under it and it will part from the stem when gently lifted upwards. Be gentle when handling and place each fruit on a layer of cotton wool in a shallow box. The fruits must not touch each other or they may decay.

After the fruit is harvested, any dead or unwanted wood is removed and the replacement shoots tied in so that they will not be broken by winter winds.

Peaches do not need pollinators to help them set fruit but on all dry days it is advisable to go over each flower with a camel hair brush. Hand pollination is a valuable assurance against crop failure, when in a cold year there are few pollinating insects about. Then, if the winds are cold or late frosts persist, hang pieces of muslin over the plants, removing them on warmer days or when the cold spell has gone.

In a warm summer, the first peaches will be ripe by mid summer; the later 'Sea Eagle' not until mid autumn, and so it is grown only in the

'Stella' dessert cherry is self-fertile which, when grown on Colt rootstock, produces a smaller tree than is traditional.

warmer parts and under glass. If in doubt about ripening, plant the early 'Duke of York' or the reliable 'Peregrine' which ripens shortly after.

VARIETIES

'BARRINGTON' An old and strong-growing peach, ripening its large pale yellow fruits in early autumn but in a sunless year tending to be too late outdoors in all but the warmest gardens. Normally grown in greenhouses.

'DUKE OF YORK' The first to ripen, this peach makes the largest fruit. It is deep crimson and of excellent flavour. The most reliable cropper if given a warm wall. Mid summer.

'EARLY RIVERS' One of the earliest, ripe by mid summer, its lemon-yellow skin and white flesh possessing excellent flavour.

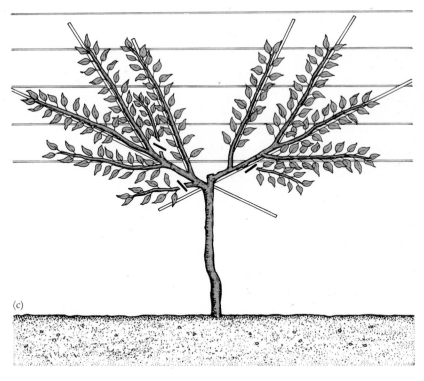

(c)

Fig. 5 (*contd.*) (*c*) First summer. Tie in new shoots to form basis of fan.

'HALE'S EARLY' By late summer, its fruit has ripened to deep orange. It bears heavy crops of medium-sized fruits of good flavour.

'PEREGRINE' Making a large crimson fruit when ripe, this matures in late summer and is a reliable cropper.

CHERRIES

For cherries to grow well and produce good crops, conditions must be right for them. In the past, they have only performed well as standard and half-standard trees, and occasionally as fans trained to walls in the large estates. These methods of growing them were so unsuited to normal-sized gardens that cherries were virtually a forgotten fruit for most gardeners.

Along with the huge size of the trees, there was also the problem of cross-pollination. There were no varieties that would set a good crop of fruit with their own pollen. All were self-sterile which meant that more than one tree had to be planted if anything like a worthwhile crop was to be produced.

As if that was not enough to put gardeners off growing them, there was also the virtual certainty that, the moment the first hint of colour came into the ripening fruit, starlings and blackbirds would swoop in and pinch the lot.

In recent years, though, much of this has changed dramatically. We now have a self-fertile variety of sweet cherry, as opposed to the acid variety 'Morello'. Also, whilst there has been no reduction in the attractiveness of the fruit to birds, we now have much smaller trees which it is possible to protect with nets.

These smaller trees are also easier to protect against spring frosts during blossom time so there is every chance that cherries will soon be grown further north than hitherto.

SOIL REQUIREMENTS

Cherries do well in a dry sunny climate. Too rich a soil causes excessive gumming when the trees are pruned and an excess of foliage with little fruit. In a lime deficient soil, work in plenty of lime rubble or mortar before planting in late autumn, allowing 6 m (20 ft) between the trees if standards. Cherries love potash, so work in to the top soil 56 g (2 oz) of sulphate of potash for each tree and each year in early spring give the trees a 28 g (1 oz) dressing.

When planting and pruning cherries, which is done in spring, take care not to damage the bark or bacterial canker or silver leaf may enter the wound causing the tree to die back. Cherries need little pruning; merely cut out any old and decayed wood and burn the prunings.

POLLINATION

It has already been said that the pollination of sweet cherries is a complicated affair. Not only does each variety, except one ('Stella'), require to be cross-pollinated but by no means all varieties are capable of pollinating each other successfully.

There are, in fact, thirteen or so groups of varieties and those within a single group will not pollinate each other. However, there are also what are called 'universal donors' which will pollinate all other varieties; the self-fertile 'Stella' is one of these.

This results in a far simpler situation whereby, if 'Stella' is grown, it can either be on its on or with any other variety and, in the latter case, both will carry full crops.

VARIETIES

'BIGARREAU NAPOLEON' A reliable variety, the large bright red fruits ripening late summer.

'EARLY RIVERS' It makes a spreading tree and bears heavily, the large jet black fruits being first to ripen in early summer. Plant it with 'Merton Heart' which will crop a month later.

'WATERLOO' A good pollinator for so many cherries hence its value but it does not bear so heavily as others. Its deep crimson fruits are ripe in mid summer.

'STELLA' The only truly self-fertile variety of sweet cherry which, even so, sets a better crop when cross-pollinated. It is a dark red cherry of good flavour ripening in mid summer.

These varieties will all pollinate each other but remember that 'Stella' is the only one that will pollinate itself.

Where cherries are grown against a wall, they will reach a height of 3 m (10 ft) or more and to the same distance on either side. After filling the wall, further shoots are removed entirely whilst all side growths are pinched back in early summer to six leaves and are again cut back to half-way early in spring.

Fruit is borne on both the old and new wood.

The acid Morello cherries, which are excellent for bottling and stewing with sugar, for they have a sharp flavour, are valuable in that they may be grown against a north wall in the fan shape. Of great hardiness, they may also be grown as low bushes or used for a hedge but since they fruit only on the new season's wood, much of the old wood is best removed early in spring. They are self-fertile and crop well without a pollinator.

ROOTSTOCKS

In the past, we have seen that cherry trees were enormous and all were grown on the common rootstock F12/1. This produced a huge tree that was quite useless for most gardens. In the late 1970s, however, a less vigorous stock named 'Colt' was introduced. This gave rise to a tree about two-thirds the size of traditional ones. Even so, this is still too large for many gardens as it means having to find room for a tree that will eventually reach some 4.5 cm (15–20 ft) high.

More recently (1986/7), a range of Belgian cherry rootstocks have been tested in the U.K. and one, 'Inmil', is being used by one nurseryman to grow sweet cherry trees for home gardeners. It is said that their ultimate height will be no more than 3 m (10 ft). These dwarfing rootstocks have yet to prove themselves here but, it they succeed, they could well bring the growing of sweet cherries within the scope of all gardeners.

PLUMS AND GAGES

Plums are the most accommodating of the stone fruits, growing well as bush and standard and half standard trees and also in the fan shape against a south or west wall. Here should be planted the gages and best dessert plums. They do well in a warm dry summer following a cold winter, the two extremes suiting plums. Being early flowering, plums should not be planted in a frost hollow. They are happier on higher ground provided they are protected from cold winds. Where frosts are experienced, plant the later-flowering varieties such as 'Oullin's Golden Gage' and 'Belle de Louvain'.

SOIL REQUIREMENTS

Plums do best in a heavy loam and like all stone fruits, do well over a chalky sub-soil. If lime is not present, give a good dressing with lime rubble or mortar before planting for in this form, lime is absorbed by the tree over a long period.

To plant a wall tree, take out a hole 46 cm (18 in) deep and place at the bottom some mortar. Spread out the roots and cover with soil to which

The mouth-watering 'Victoria' plum is ideal for gardens. The trees are relatively small and no pollinators are required.

has been added either some decayed manure, or a handful of bone meal. The stem should be 15 cm (6 in) from the wall and make sure that the union is 8 cm (3 in) above the surface when the soil has been filled in and made firm. Late autumn is the best time to plant and in mid spring give the plants 28 g (1 oz) dressing of sulphate of potash. Above all, give a thick mulch each year in early summer. This will provide the plant with nitrogen and help to conserve moisture in the soil without which wall plants will not do well. Plums make considerable growth and are copious drinkers. They will soon reach a height of 3 m (10 ft) and the same in width and bear fruit all along the wood. The shoots are tied to the wall about 23 cm (9 in) apart.

Very little pruning is needed and, if necessary, it is done in early spring as the tree comes into life after its winter rest, when the cuts heal quickly and it is much less likely to admit the Silver Leaf fungus. Pruning consists of the removal of dead wood and shortening unduly long shoots which must be burnt. Early in summer, side shoots are pinched back to encourage the formation of fruiting spurs.

Some plums are self-fertile and will set fruit with their own pollen; others are only partly so; and some are self-sterile and set fruit only with a pollinator. However, all will set heavier crops where provided with a pollinator. Plums flower only for 18–20 days and apart from those which bloom very early and others very late, most will overlap but as they bloom for a shorter time than any other fruit, they may be seriously harmed by frost.

VARIETIES

RIPE MID-LATE SUMMER
'CZAR' Resistant to frost for it blooms late yet matures early, cropping well in exposed gardens. The bright purple fruit can be used for cooking by mid summer, for dessert late summer.
'DENNISTON'S SUPERB' This is used as a pollinator for many plums and gages and is ripe late summer, the round gage-like fruits being deep green, flushed with crimson and with the true gage flavour.

RIPE LATE SUMMER
'OULLIN'S GOLDEN GAGE' The best gage for this time, its round fruits ripening to golden yellow. It blooms late and is valuable for gardens troubled by frost.
'VICTORIA' The most vigorous and heavy-cropping of all plums. It is self-fertile and pollinates many varieties. Like 'Czar', it crops well in clay soils, its large egg-shaped fruits ripening to pinkish-red.

'CAMBRIDGE GAGE' A true greengage colour of green fading to yellow with a light russet. The flesh is rich and juicy and the flavour excellent. First-rate for dessert but makes rather a sweet and sickly jam.

RIPE IN EARLY AUTUMN
'BRYANSTON GAGE' This makes a large tree and crops well in fan-shape, bearing in early autumn, round greenish fruits speckled with russet.

RIPE IN MID AUTUMN
'MARJORIE'S SEEDLING' A deep purple almost black plum with a light bloom and russet streaks. Flesh is yellow, rather mealy and sharp. Used mainly for cooking. Partially self-fertile. Vigorous and upright tree. Resistant to bacterial canker and silver leaf diseases.

DAMSONS

Extremely hardy, damsons crop well in the most exposed gardens and may be planted as a wind break. They also crop well in shallow, stony ground and are rarely troubled by frosts. Plant 2.5–3 m (8–10 ft) apart and do no pruning apart from the occasional removal of dead wood.

The best variety is 'Merryweather' for it sets its own fruit which ripens in early October to blue-black and is of large size. When stewed, it has the true damson flavour. It makes a broad spreading tree.

A blackberry/raspberry hybrid from Scotland, the recently bred tayberry crops far more heavily and is much hardier than the similar loganberry.

CHAPTER 9

PESTS AND DISEASES

APPLES

PESTS

APHIS (GREENFLY) The green insects attack all fruits and lay their eggs on the plants where they winter, emerging in spring to feed on the young shoots and causing leaf curl. Spray with tar-oil in mid winter, or in mid spring with a systemic insecticide and again in early summer.

APPLE SUCKER This resembles the greenfly and lays and feeds on the fruit spurs in autumn, later on the flower buds causing them to turn brown. The eggs are destroyed by tar-oil in mid winter, or spray with a systemic insecticide in mid spring.

BLOSSOM WEEVIL The grubs eat into the flower buds early in summer so that they fail to open. The black insects winter in the bark. Spraying with tar-oil should give control.

CODLING MOTH This is responsible for the maggoty condition of mature apples, its presence indicated by a pile of brown dirt at the point of entry when the fruit will be riddled with holes right through. The moth lays its eggs in early and mid summer. To prevent an attack, spray the trees in mid summer with Fentro (based on fenitrothion), Picket or Sybol.

TORTRIX MOTH The caterpillars attack apples and pears, causing the leaves to curl up at the edges. Defoliation occurs whilst the grubs weave a silken web over the flowers which die. It is one of the most destructive of fruit pests. As routine, spray in late spring and again in early mid summer as for codling moth.

WINTER MOTH Hibernating in the soil, these make their way up the tree stem in mid-winter and if unchecked, feed on the blossom and leaves. About mid summer, they fall to the ground to pupate, the moths emerg-

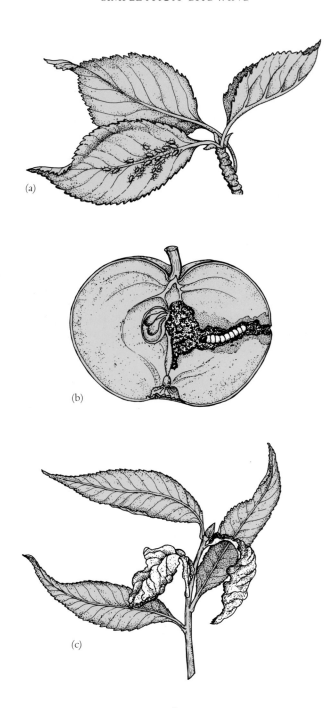

ing in winter. Grease-banding the trees in early autumn will trap many. As an additional precaution, spray with tar-oil in mid winter.

WOOLLY APHIS Also known as American Blight, this produces a grey, woolly substance under the branches where the pests winter and lay their eggs in spring, causing the branches to swell and crack. Spray with tar-oil in mid winter or with systemic insecticide in green-bud stage.

DISEASES

BROWN ROT This occurs on the fruiting spurs as brown spots causing them to die back whilst the fruit will turn brown in storage. Burn all diseased fruits and spray with a systemic fungicide such as Benlate whilst the buds are still green in early spring and again a fortnight later.

CANKER This attacks all top fruits but mostly those growing in badly drained soil, appearing as cracked and rough lesions which may encircle a branch, causing it to die back at this point. 'Bramley's' and 'Grenadier' are highly resistant. To control, remove the entire branch, if girdled, at the point of intersection with the main stem and treat the wound with Arbrex or Seal and Heal.

SCAB This attacks apples and pears given too much nitrogen, appearing on fruit and leaves as brown spots and is most active in a wet season. It winters on fallen fruits and prunings which should be burnt. To prevent, spray with a systemic fungicide at green-bud stage, and at fortnightly intervals until mid summer.

BLACKBERRY AND LOGANBERRY

PESTS

APHIS The insects sometimes collect on the tips of the shoots (canes) or cluster beneath the leaves, sucking the sap and reducing the vitality of the plants. To prevent damage, spray with systemic insecticide when seen.

Fig. 6(a) (*Opposite*) Greenfly may start to appear as early as mid-spring. Treat them as soon as you see any. (b) Codling moth caterpillar damage. Avoid maggoty apples by spraying twice, two weeks apart, with permethrin during mid-summer. (c) Peach leaf curl. A difficult disease to control. Spray with Bordeaux mixture at leaf-fall and in early spring.

RASPBERRY BEETLE See under Raspberry.

DISEASE

CANE SPOT The most troublesome disease affecting both old and new wood, causing it to break off and the fruit buds to fall off before opening. To prevent, spray Benlate at bud burst and just before blossom.

BLACK CURRANT

PESTS

GALL MITE The most troublesome pest which causes Big Bud. Where present, the mite is there in thousands though visible only through a microscope, the buds being swollen with them. The only cure is to remove the swollen buds during the winter and burn them.

GREEN CAPSID BUG The eggs winter on older plants and hatch out in mid spring, the bugs feeding on the leaves and buds. It is killed with tar-oil in mid winter.

LEAF MIDGE It is present when the leaf edges roll up and here the midges lay their eggs. Spray with systemic insecticide when first flowers open and again three weeks later.

DISEASES

LEAF SPOT In a wet year, this may attack the stems and foliage as brown spots, causing the leaves to fall prematurely. To control, spray with systemic fungicide after picking the fruit.
RUST This appears as orange spots under the leaves causing them to fall and the plant to lose vitality. After picking the fruit, spray with Bordeaux mixture.

CHERRY

PESTS

FRUIT MOTH The small green caterpillars enter the buds as they open and later, bore into the fruits making them unusable. The moths emerge from the chrysalid state in mid summer and lay their eggs on the leaves. To prevent an attack, spray with tar-oil in mid winter or with Picket just before the blossom opens.

Greenfly (aphids), if left untreated, will soon distort shoots and weaken the whole tree by feeding on the sap.

RED SPIDER   See under Plum.

DISEASES

BACTERIAL CANKER   The disease occurs as yellow circles on the leaves which curl up and as 'gumming' of any wounds. The bacteria will spread on to the stems causing them to die back. It is destructive so spray with Bordeaux mixture in late autumn and again in early spring.

CANKER   See under Apple.

SILVER LEAF   See under Plum.

(d)

Fig. 6 (*contd.*) (*d*) Gooseberry sawfly caterpillars can soon defoliate a bush. Watch for them from mid-spring onwards and spray with permethrin.

GOOSEBERRY

PESTS

APHIS See under Raspberry

SAWFLY The most troublesome gooseberry pest, attacking and skeletonizing the leaves in spring and early summer. Spray with Malathion or Sybol when first seen.

DISEASES

GREY MOULD (BOTRYTIS) See also under Strawberries. With gooseberries, it attacks the new shoots and leaves causing them to die back which is its other name. It is most prevalent in a wet season or where the plants have grown 'soft' with too much nitrogen in the soil. To prevent, spray with Benlate as the flowers open.

LEAF SPOT This often appears after a wet season, or where the soil is waterlogged, as brown spots on the leaves, causing them to fall prematurely. To control, spray with systemic fungicide after gathering the fruit.

PEACH

PESTS

APHIS   See under Apple.

MEALY BUG   See under Vine.

RED SPIDER   See under Plum.

SCALE   The insects cluster on the stems like brown scales where they suck the sap reducing the vitality of the plant. To prevent, spray with tar-oil in early winter or with systemic insecticide in early spring.

DISEASES

BACTERIAL CANKER   See under Cherry.

LEAF CURL   The most troublesome of peach diseases, usually appearing in a wet year, the fungus attacking the leaves, causing the edges to curl and redden before turning brown and dying, later spreading to the stems when the tree will lose vitality. To prevent, spray early in spring and straight after leaf fall with Bordeaux mixture or Benlate.

Fig. 6   (*contd.*) (*e*) Apple scab is a disfiguring fungus disease. Spray every 10–14 days with Benlate when first seen.

(e)

When apple mildew attacks the blossom like this, no fruits will be produced. The cluster should be picked off and destroyed.

Brown rot of plums is perpetuated by diseased fruits overwintering on the branches; pick them off and burn them.

PEAR

PESTS

BLOSSOM WEEVIL See under Apple.

CODLING MOTH See under Apple.

LEAF BLISTER MIDGE These attack the leaves and fruits causing reddish-brown blisters to appear, beneath which the eggs are laid. The mites are invisible to the eye and winter in the bud scales. To control, spray with systemic fungicide in mid spring.

PEAR MIDGE Eggs are laid on the blossom in mid spring (late flowering varieties seem to escape), the maggots tunnelling into the fruit. Afterwards they fall to the ground to pupate in the soil. Spray the tree with Fentro in spring.

TORTRIX MOTH See under Apple.

WINTER MOTH See under Apple.

DISEASES

CANKER See under Apple.

SCAB Biologically different from Apple Scab and each cannot affect the other. It affects the shoots as black blisters and later the fruits. Control as for Apple Scab.

PLUM

PESTS

RED SPIDER This also attacks damsons and peaches, particularly where growing against a wall. The red insects with spider-like legs cluster on the underside of the leaves sucking the sap. To control, spray plums, damsons, peaches and apricots with systemic insecticide in early summer and repeat as necessary.

RED PLUM MAGGOT It is this that causes maggots to be in mature plums during the summer and autumn. Soak, especially the trunks, with tar oil winter wash in mid winter.

MEALY PLUM APHID Colonies of powdery greenfly seen from early summer onwards on the ends of the new shoots. Spray with systemic insecticide when first seen.

DISEASES

BROWN ROT See under Apple.

CANKER See under Apple.

SILVER LEAF Most serious of plum and cherry diseases, the foliage turning a silver colour and soon the tree will die back entirely. The two most prolific croppers, 'Czar' and 'Victoria' are the most susceptible. Prune only during spring and summer, to allow the trees time to close up the wounds which they will not do in winter. Nor does the fungus spread during the growing season.

RASPBERRY

PESTS

APHIS The insects penetrate the stems causing virus diseases to enter. Their presence is noted by swellings on the canes. A tar-oil wash in mid winter controls, or spray with systemic insecticide when seen.

RASPBERRY BEETLE The most troublesome of raspberry pests, the tiny grey beetle lays her eggs in the flowers, the white grubs later feeding on the fruits and remaining on them after picking. They are always present and as routine, spray with malathion or Picket when the fruit begins to colour.

RASPBERRY MOTH This winters in the soil at the base of the canes, emerging from a cocoon in spring as a silvery-brown moth. It lays in the blossom like the Beetle, the grubs feeding on the fruits. To prevent, soak the soil around the canes with tar-oil in mid winter.

DISEASES

CANE BLIGHT Similar to Cane Spot, but it attacks the canes at soil level causing them to wilt and die. There is no specific cure but spraying the base of the canes with Benlate is helpful.

CANE SPOT A fungus which attacks young canes showing as purple markings in summer, causing the canes to die back to the infected part. To prevent, spray with Benlate as leaf burst and repeat fortnightly until after flowering.

MOSAIC A virus disease introduced by aphis and present in the sap causing the leaves to turn yellow. If noticed, pull up and burn infected canes for there is no cure. If experienced, plant aphid resistant varieties.

RED CURRANT

PESTS

CLEARWING MOTH This lays its eggs along the branches and upon hatching, the grubs penetrate the stems causing them to die back. Routine spraying in winter with tar-oil will prevent an outbreak.

STRAWBERRY

PESTS

APHIS The most troublesome of strawberry pests, feeding on the sap and reducing the vitality of the plant whilst spreading virus diseases. Their presence is denoted by the curled leaves. To prevent, spray with systemic insecticide in spring before the blossom opens.

BLOSSOM WEEVIL These lay their eggs in the blossom, feeding on the pollen and causing the flowers to be unfruitful. To prevent, dust the flower trusses with derris powder when opening and again 14 days later.

TARSONEMID MITE The mites begin to lay their eggs in the heart of the plants when the new leaves unfold in spring. Spray them with a systemic insecticide. This will also give some control against red spider. Well-drained soil in good heart will usually prevent the plants being troubled by pests or diseases.

DISEASES

BOTRYTIS (GREY MOULD) This is the all too common disease which causes the fruits to rot and become covered with fungus. It is particularly bad in a wet year. Spray fortnightly with Benlate from when first flower opens until picking is over.

INDEX